OUTDOOR RECREATION AREAS

Other Publications:

AMERICAN COUNTRY
VOYAGE THROUGH THE UNIVERSE
THE THIRD REICH
THE TIME-LIFE GARDENER'S GUIDE
MYSTERIES OF THE UNKNOWN
TIME FRAME
FIX IT YOURSELF
FITNESS, HEALTH & NUTRITION
SUCCESSFUL PARENTING
HEALTHY HOME COOKING
UNDERSTANDING COMPUTERS
LIBRARY OF NATIONS
THE ENCHANTED WORLD
THE KODAK LIBRARY OF CREATIVE PHOTOGRAPHY
GREAT MEALS IN MINUTES
THE CIVIL WAR
PLANET EARTH
COLLECTOR'S LIBRARY OF THE CIVIL WAR
THE EPIC OF FLIGHT
THE GOOD COOK
WORLD WAR II
THE OLD WEST

For information on and a full description of any of the
Time-Life Books series listed above, please call
1-800-621-7026 or write:
Reader Information
Time-Life Customer Service
P.O. Box C-32068
Richmond, Virginia 23261-2068

This volume is part of a series offering homeowners
detailed instructions on repairs, construction and
improvements they can undertake themselves.

HOME REPAIR
AND IMPROVEMENT

OUTDOOR RECREATION AREAS

BY THE EDITORS OF
TIME-LIFE BOOKS

TIME-LIFE BOOKS
ALEXANDRIA, VIRGINIA

Time-Life Books Inc.
is a wholly owned subsidiary of
TIME INCORPORATED

Founder Henry R. Luce 1898-1967
Editor-in-Chief Jason McManus
Chairman and Chief Executive Officer J. Richard Munro
President and Chief Operating Officer N. J. Nicholas Jr.
Editorial Director Ray Cave
Executive Vice President, Books Kelso F. Sutton
Vice President, Books Paul V. McLaughlin

TIME-LIFE BOOKS INC.

Editor George Constable
Executive Editor Ellen Phillips
Director of Design Louis Klein
Director of Editorial Resources Phyllis K. Wise
Editorial Board Russell B. Adams Jr., Dale M. Brown, Roberta Conlan, Thomas H. Flaherty, Lee Hassig, Donia Ann Steele, Rosalind Stubenberg
Director of Photography and Research John Conrad Weiser
Assistant Director of Editorial Resources Elise Ritter Gibson

President Christopher T. Linen
Chief Operating Officer John M. Fahey Jr.
Senior Vice Presidents Robert M. DeSena, James L. Mercer, Paul R. Stewart
Vice Presidents Stephen L. Bair, Ralph J. Cuomo, Neal Goff, Stephen L. Goldstein, Juanita T. James, Hallett Johnson III, Carol Kaplan, Susan J. Maruyama, Robert H. Smith,
Director of Production Services Joseph J. Ward
Supervisor of Quality Control Robert J. Passantino
James King

HOME REPAIR AND IMPROVEMENT
Editorial Staff for Outdoor Recreation Areas

Editor Robert M. Jones
Assistant Editors Betsy Frankel, Brooke Stoddard
Designer Edward Frank
Chief Researcher Oobie Gleysteen
Picture Editor Neil Kagan
Associate Designer Kenneth E. Hancock
Text Editors Leslie Marshall, Katherine Miller
Staff Writers Lynn R. Addison, Patricia Bangs, William C. Banks, Megan Barnett, Michael Blumenthal, Robert A. Doyle, Steven J. Forbis, Peter Pocock, William Worsley
Copy Coordinator Margery duMond
Art Associates George Bell, Lorraine D. Rivard, Richard Whiting
Editorial Assistant Susan Larson

Editorial Operations

Copy Chief Diane Ullius
Production Celia Beattie
Library Louise D. Forstall

Correspondents: Elisabeth Kraemer-Singh (Bonn); Maria Vincenza Aloisi (Paris); Ann Natanson (Rome). Valuable assistance was also provided by: Enid Farmer (Boston); Diane Asselin (Los Angeles); Judy Aspinall, Karin B. Pearce (London); Carolyn T. Chubet, Miriam Hsia, Christina Lieberman (New York); Sandra Hinson (Orlando, Fla.); Mimi Murphy (Rome); Carol Barnard (Seattle).

THE CONSULTANTS: Dave Kaiser is a freelance writer and editor of publications on swimming pools and pool construction, among them *Swimming Pool Weekly/Age Data and Reference Annual* and *Swimming Pools, a Guide to Their Planning, Design and Operation* for the Council for National Cooperation in Aquatics. He is also managing editor of a number of Saudi Arabian periodicals.

Richard J. Lewis, a landscape construction contractor for more than two decades, has designed and built many landscaping projects for private homes, parks, schools and commercial establishments.

Sheldon Westervelt is a consultant on tennis-court design and construction for court builders in the United States, Europe, South America and Japan. He has written numerous articles on court construction for such magazines as *Tennis*, *World Tennis* and *Tennis Industry*.

Roswell W. Ard, a civil engineer, is a consulting structural engineer and a professional home inspector who has written professional papers on wood-frame construction techniques. He has designed heating, electrical and motor-control systems, and has explored alternate energy systems, including solar-energy and wind-power generators.

Harris Mitchell, special consultant for Canada, has worked in the field of home repair and improvement for more than two decades. He is Homes editor of *Today* magazine and author of a syndicated newspaper column, "You Wanted to Know," as well as a number of books on home improvement.

Mark M. Steele, consultant for the revised edition of this volume, is a professional home inspector in the Washington, D.C., area and an editor of home improvement articles and books.

Time-Life Books Inc. offers a wide range of fine recordings, including a *Rock 'n' Roll Era* series. For subscription information, call 1-800-621-7026 or write Time-Life Music, P.O. Box C-32068, Richmond, Virginia 23261-2068.

Library of Congress Cataloging in Publication Data
Outdoor recreation areas / by the editors of Time-Life Books.—Rev. ed.
  p. cm.—(Home repair and improvement)
  Includes index
ISBN 0-8094-7354-2
ISBN 0-8094-7355-0 (lib. bdg.)
1. Recreation areas—Equipment and supplies.
2. Outdoor recreation—Equipment and supplies.
3. Recreation areas—Design and construction.
4. Recreation areas—Maintenance and repair.
I. Time-Life Books.   II. Series
GV182.5.O95 1989
790.1'91—dc19   83-36629 CIP

Contents

COLOR PORTFOLIO: Offbeat Approaches to Child's Play   72

1   Planning for Play—within Limits   **7**
How to Evaluate Potential Recreation Space   8
Changing the Lay of the Land for Sports   14
A Retaining Wall to Hold a Hill   19
Fast Drainage to Keep Your Play Area Dry   22

2   Play Surfaces Suited to the Game   **25**
Natural Advantages of Grass: Tough, Soft, Springy   26
Constructing a Base for a Good Tennis Court   32
Choosing a Surface for the Court   38
An Ice-Skating Rink from a Garden Hose   44

3   Preparing for Diverse Diversions   **49**
Posts and Poles: The Basic Support System   50
Outdoor Lights to Lengthen the Period of Play   54
The Dividers and Barricades: Nets and Fences   60
A Playhouse of Modular Panels   68
A Backyard Gym with a Variety of Attractions   82

4   The Joys of Water, Cool or Hot   **95**
How to Assemble and Install an Above-ground Pool   96
Hot Tubs: A Bit of Rome at Home   102
A Wood Deck for Hot Tub or Pool   107
The Best of Care for an Above- or In-ground Pool   112
Keeping Water Chemically Pure   115
Preparing a Pool for Winter Cold   121
Tapping Nature for a Fishing Pond All Your Own   124
Building Lake Floats for Docking or Diving   126

Appendix: Laying Out Courts and Fields   **130**

Acknowledgments and Picture Credits   **134**

Index/Glossary   **135**

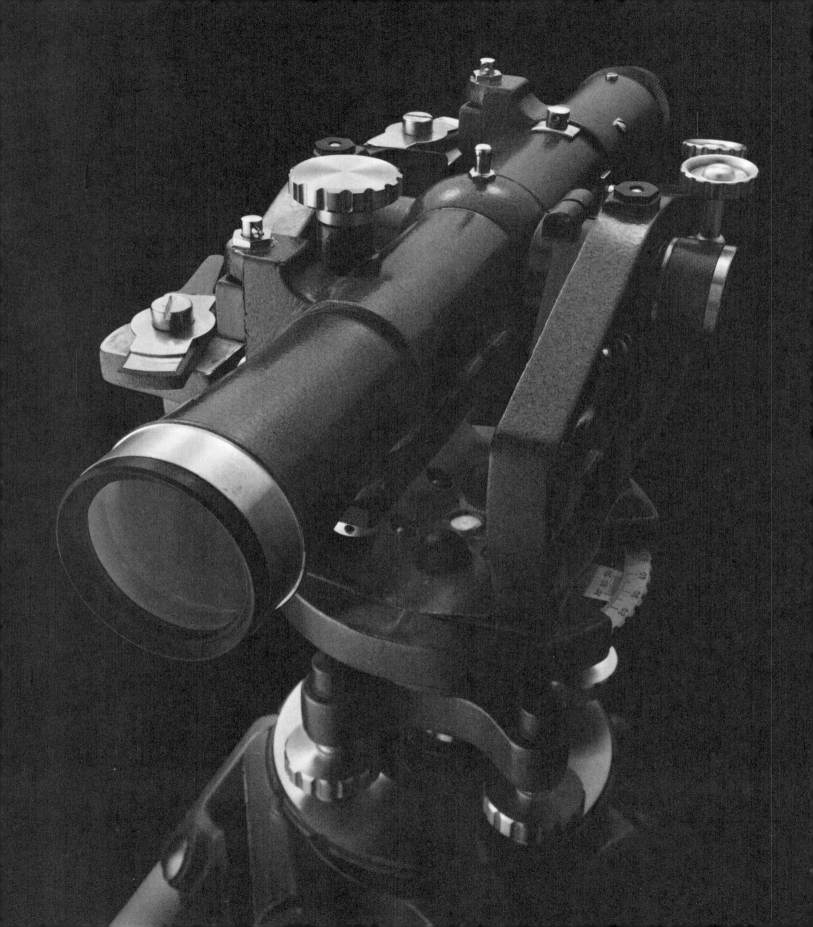

Planning for Play—within Limits

An improved eye for the excavator. In preparing a recreation site, a rented transit level has two functions: It is used to set precise boundaries for courts and playing fields and to measure the grade if you need to modify the surface.

If you were to draw a rough sketch of your house and yard and mark the areas where you spend most of your leisure hours, you probably would find that almost all pleasure activity takes place in less than 10 per cent of the available space; indeed, it may even be confined to one or two rooms in the house and a few square feet outside. By evaluating your house and land imaginatively and planning carefully for new outdoor recreation areas, you can create more living space and dramatically increase your enjoyment of free time at home.

Because enlarging the yard itself is usually unfeasible, you need to concentrate on making the most of existing space. There are many ways to expand the usable area within a given set of boundaries. Trees and shrubs can be removed or relocated, slopes can be terraced with retaining walls to make level play areas, swampy land can be drained and filled.

Such changes will inevitably affect your neighbors, so keep a good-neighbor policy in mind. Try to shield the house next door from lighted play areas and locate any noisy zone, like a basketball court, where the sound will be least disturbing. If structural parts of a fence are visible on one side, build the fence so its more attractive side faces outward. Consult your neighbors before building any fence, to avoid later ill feeling; a neighbor may even share the cost if the fence is built along a common property line.

Beyond such responsibilities, legal liability may be a factor in building any outdoor structure that could be deemed, in legal jargon, an "attractive nuisance." By law, the simple presence in your yard of an unprotected structure that attracts uninvited visitors may make you liable for injuries that result from its use.

Major outdoor improvements are investments. In most areas, a permanent improvement such as an in-ground pool increases the value of a house—and its tax assessment. (An above-ground pool usually is considered portable personal property.) Permanent pools and tennis courts are often assessed upon completion and taxed on the basis of square feet of surface, although in some areas no tax is added until the house is reassessed. But note that recreation improvements do not always raise the resale value of property—that depends on how attractive they are to the buyer.

Stated simply, the success of new recreational space will rest on your ability to determine beforehand the most exciting possibilities for your yard within the existing physical, legal and financial limits. Whether you want your new yard to be a secluded oasis in a busy world, or to attract friends for entertainment and sport, you will save time as well as money through thoughtful and comprehensive planning from the beginning.

How to Evaluate Potential Recreation Space

Planning a home recreation area begins with three basic considerations: who will be using the space, when it will be used, and how it will be used most often. An area that is to be used primarily by adults for evening badminton will need elements very different from those required in an area that will be used mainly by children for daytime play.

However, determining the primary use need not mean excluding other activities. In fact, the multiple use of any space is a desirable objective. A free-play area cleared for young softball players can accommodate adult volleyball as well. A hard-surfaced tennis court provides a mud-free area for roller skating or tricycle riding. A basketball hoop mounted over a driveway may convert that wasted space into a much-used practice area.

In addition to planning alternative uses of space at different times of the day and in different seasons of the year, try to formulate a master plan for the future. Young trees that you plant along the edge of a play area for small children can be selected and placed so that, as they grow, they will form a windbreak for more sophisticated games later. A playground covered with sand, bark or pine needles to cushion children's tumbles from a climbing gym may become a small ice-skating rink in later years, and the same area may even provide a good start for a rose garden some day.

When you have thought about the kinds of recreation areas you and your family would enjoy, study your land to determine whether the plan is feasible. First measure your property. At the time of purchase, most homeowners receive a plot map that sets forth the exact boundaries of their land. If you do not have such a map, the city or county zoning office may have plot maps on file. If not, have your land surveyed to establish precise boundaries; your deed will contain a legal description of where they lie.

Become familiar with local zoning laws and building codes, and check your deed to discover whether there are any restrictions on the use of the property. Zoning laws may prohibit certain types of outdoor construction. Building codes may specify the types of fences you can build, or the type you must build around a swimming pool. Easements for sidewalks or water or sewer lines may limit the amount of land you can use for certain purposes. Finally, check with your local homeowners' association to find out if there are any neighborhood understandings about outdoor structures.

You should be able to learn from utility companies the locations of any underground power, gas, water or sewer lines that might interfere with projects that require digging. If you have a septic system, locate the tank and the drain tiles in the leaching field before you plan any earth-moving or posthole digging.

The best place to begin an evaluation of your yard is inside the house. Study the views from the windows, so you can take care not to block or mar an attractive view if you build a new fence or playground. Note how doors will be used to gain access to play areas, and whether dirt might be tracked in where it will be most conspicuous. If you have small children, consider whether you will want to supervise their play more often from the kitchen or from the living room.

As you plan, keep convenience and easy maintenance in mind. Locating a child's outdoor play area near indoor play space can save many steps at dusk as toys are retrieved. Worn areas of lawn suggest established traffic patterns that you may prefer not to interrupt with new plantings or fences. When you lay out grass playing areas, note that narrow or odd-shaped pieces of lawn may prove difficult to mow and trim.

Grading and earth-moving should be completed before construction or planting begins. If your plans call for the use of heavy machinery, establish access routes. For example, such equipment should never be driven within a tree's drip line, as defined by the tips of its outermost branches; compaction of the earth around the roots might kill the tree. Nor should it be driven close to the house, where it might damage the foundation, or over a septic field, where it might crush the tiles.

Local weather conditions can help you choose a site for recreation facilities. Sun and wind can be screened with judicious planting or fencing, of course (page 66). But give thought to other influences on the temperature in your yard. For instance, masonry patios and walls absorb heat during the day and radiate it long after the sun has set. The cool evening air of spring and fall will tend to pool in any enclosed, low-lying area; you can retain it or spill it out by controlling any gaps left in the fence or hedge that surrounds that area. To help keep midsummer-afternoon temperatures bearable, locate a play space where trees will provide cooling shade, or plant vines that will cover walls and fences.

Recreation areas are primarily functional, but esthetic considerations are not unimportant. While a single floodlight might be enough to illuminate a yard for evening croquet, a few strategically placed shielded lights set among bushes and shrubs enhance the romance of the game. And stroll around your yard, pausing to listen for any unpleasant noise that you might have learned to ignore. Fences and plantings can be used to baffle such noise. Even the sound of running water in a fountain serves to disguise traffic roar. Should unpleasant odors encroach, fragrant shrubs and herbs can provide a surprising amount of pleasant perfume.

Examining the yard. Walk slowly around your property, noting first those major features that must be regarded as permanent: an outcropping of bedrock, large shade trees, your house and the houses of neighbors, the directional orientation. Next evaluate features that could be changed: small trees and rocks, shrubs, fences, areas that could be opened up or enclosed. Examine the land itself. A visible slope will tell you the direction of drainage, which is important if new grading will be needed to create a level space or to fill in a swampy area. Finally, consider the invisible features: underground pipes, easements, composition of the soil, even the drip line around a large tree.

GAS MAIN
WATER MAIN
EASEMENT
DRAINAGE PIPE
TOPSOIL
SUBSOIL
SWAMPY AREA

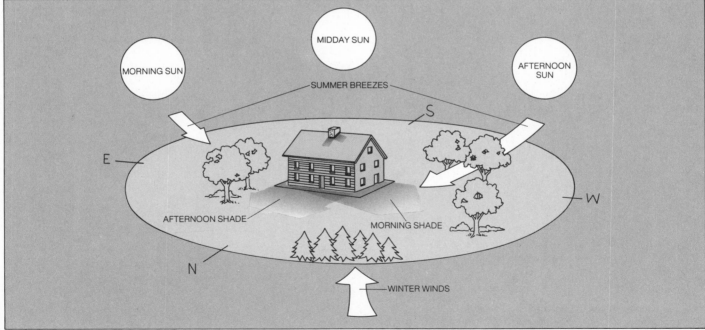

MORNING SUN
MIDDAY SUN
AFTERNOON SUN
SUMMER BREEZES
S
E
W
N
AFTERNOON SHADE
MORNING SHADE
WINTER WINDS

Evaluating sun and wind. Note the effects of sun and wind in your yard. Warming sunlight might be welcome on the patio on a summer morning, but blazing afternoon sun would have to be screened out with trees, tall shrubs or a fence. Observe where shadows fall and the effect they have during the hours of primary recreational use in all seasons.

In the Northern Hemisphere, summer breezes usually come from the southeast or southwest, while cold winter winds are usually northerly. But your area may have unusual wind patterns; consult your local weather bureau. If cooling summer breezes are blocked by lower tree branches, prune the branches off. But if winter winds are discomforting, they should be blunted with a windbreak of evergreen trees or fencing.

Measuring the yard. Use the side of the house as a giant straightedge to determine the relative distances and locations of various landscape features such as trees and rocks. Hold the end of a 50- or 100-foot steel tape against the side of the house, 10 feet in from a corner, while a helper extends the tape to a point in the yard where it forms a right angle with a line to the object whose location you are measuring. Sight down the side of the house to make sure the tape is straight, and have your helper mark the point with a stake. Measure the distance from the house to the stake by subtracting the 10 feet of house wall used in sighting. Then place a steel square against the stake to establish an exact right angle, and measure to the object.

In the same fashion, locate other objects with reference to the house. In some cases you may be able to line up the object with the house wall directly, without establishing a reference point and right angle. Use these measurements and the dimensions of the house to plot a rough map of the yard (*opposite, top*).

STEEL SQUARE

Measuring changes in grade. Rest a hand-held sighting level (*inset*) atop a 5-foot pole—a 1-by-2 is adequate—and sight horizontally to a second pole held upright by a helper 50 feet away. The second pole should be calibrated at 6-inch intervals with marks bold enough to read at a distance. Take a reading on the second pole and subtract from it the 5-foot height of the sighting pole, to get the change in elevation between the two poles. Take similar readings along the length and width of the area to be used for recreational purposes, and note the measurements on your rough map.

A change in elevation of 1 foot in 50 feet amounts to a grade of 2 per cent. This is flat enough for informal play areas, such as a volleyball court, and at the same time its slope (although imperceptible to the eye) provides adequate drainage. In most cases the maximum slope for informal games is 5 per cent.

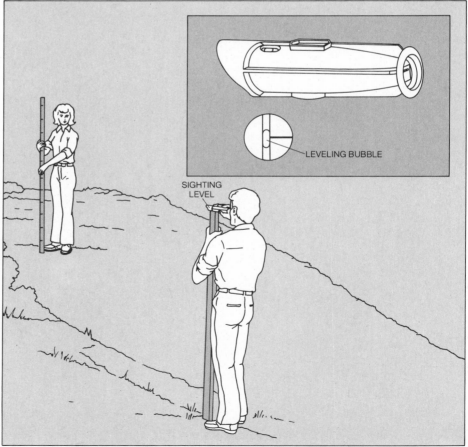

LEVELING BUBBLE

SIGHTING LEVEL

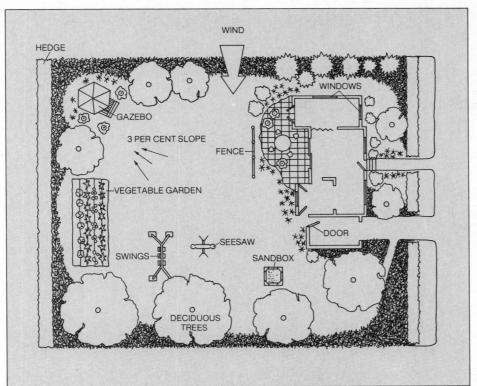

Drawing a grid map. Plot all major landscape features on graph paper, using the measurements taken earlier. Choose a convenient scale: For a small property, one grid square can equal 1 foot; for larger properties, one square may have to represent 4 or 5 feet to allow you to fit the map on one sheet of paper. When drawing the house, mark the position of windows and doors to help you calculate the visibility of play areas from the house and the access to them. Note significant changes of grade; indicate the direction of prevailing winds and the seasonal variation in the angle of the sun.

When the map is complete, cut out paper or cardboard templates representing scale models of planned play areas and equipment, and move them around on the map until you find the most suitable locations for them.

Building mock-ups. To better visualize the effects of planned outdoor structures, create full-sized mock-ups, using stakes and twine to define their dimensions. If the structure will affect the view or cast a shadow, drape sheets or newspapers over the string and note how shadows affect the playing area during the time of day when you will most often use it.

If you intend to install outdoor lighting, tie flashlights to poles or tree branches to suggest the effect of night lighting on the playing area—as well as on your neighbor's property.

Testing the soil. Obtain a test sample of the soil beneath a planned recreation area by driving a 3-foot length of 1½-inch pipe into the ground with a small sledge. When the pipe has penetrated about 2 feet, rock it back and forth until you can pull it out. Use a broomstick or a 1-inch dowel to push the soil slowly out of the pipe into an orderly row on a sheet of newspaper. By examining the row, you can see roughly how deep the topsoil is. Take samples at several places; note on your plot plan where each came from.

To check the topsoil type, moisten it slightly and feel it. Sandy loam feels gritty; clay loam feels sticky and smooth and when pressed into a ribbon will hold that shape. (Loam is a mixture of sand and clay in various proportions, plus organic matter.) Generally, sandy loam drains quickly and is more desirable for a playing field. Clay loam absorbs and releases water slowly and is more likely to heave and contract as water content changes. If you plan extensive construction, have your soil analyzed by an expert.

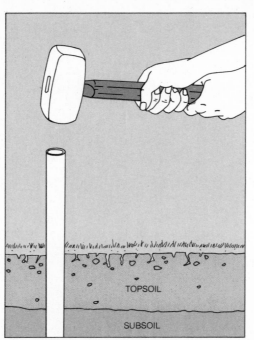

TOPSOIL

SUBSOIL

Checking a swimming area. To evaluate an untried natural swimming area, probe the bottom near the shore with a long pole marked at 1-foot intervals to measure depth. Note especially any sharp drop-offs that could endanger waders.

Have a strong swimmer, wearing a face mask, swim fins and work gloves, examine the bottom in wading areas. If you find slimy mud, signs of heavy vegetation, or sharp rocks, you may want to cover the bottom with sand in shallow areas.

Check for large underwater obstacles such as rocks or tree branches and remove them if possible. Observe the movement of floating debris for signs of a strong current.

Examine the shoreline for evidence of erosion. A bank that is more than 3 or 4 feet above the surface of the water often indicates that waves and ice are wearing away the land. Toppled earth with green foliage still attached to it usually signals recent and rapid erosion. Stacking large rocks in the water near the bank will slow such erosion in many cases.

A Yard that Reflects Evolving Patterns of Play

1 **A modest beginning.** The recreation space in this yard primarily suits the needs of small children. A sandbox and swings are in a shady area clearly visible from the kitchen. Low fences and shrubs surround the yard and limit access to the street. Even with trees in the middle of the lawn, there is adequate free-play space. The patio is large enough for family use and provides a surface where children can use wheeled toys.

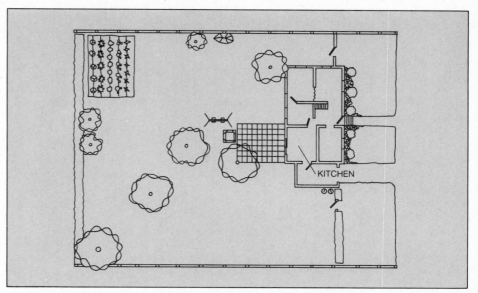

2 **Expanding outdoor activity.** As the children grow older, trees in the center of the yard have been removed to provide more open space for organized games. The patio has been extended, increasing space for outdoor entertaining. A new parking area in the driveway doubles as a basketball practice court. In a back corner of the yard, a fence and hedge have been added, separating the enlarged vegetable garden and a new tool shed from the play area. The tree in the opposite back corner is now large enough to accommodate a tree house, and several young shade trees have been planted to give increased privacy. The swing set has been replaced by a climbing gym, and the sandbox, moved closer to the house, is now a planter.

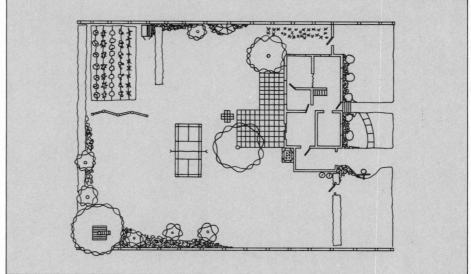

3 **Recreation geared for adults.** The shade trees planted earlier have grown to provide both privacy and a windbreak for a tennis court. To make room for the court, the size of the garden has been reduced. Shrubs give privacy for a hot tub that is surrounded by a deck and screened by foliage. Across the yard, a large rock serves as the foundation for a sun deck. The climbing gym has been removed. The basketball hoop has been taken down since an increased number of drivers makes it likely that a car will usually be parked in the driveway.

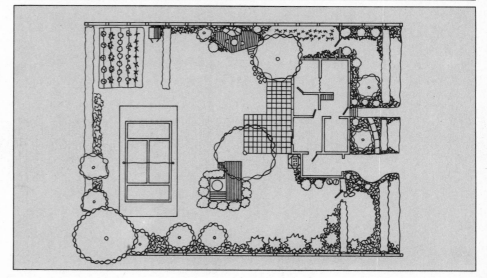

Changing the Lay of the Land for Sports

Many sports lovers—and spectators—are under the impression that the perfect tennis or volleyball court is absolutely flat. In fact, the ideal playing surface slopes slightly so that water will drain off quickly. If a proposed site is really flat, puddles will collect on it after a rain, and it will have to be graded.

Indeed, grading is probably the most common task in preparing any recreational site. You can even carve a playing field from such an unpromising site as a scarred, steeply sloped hillside—provided you are willing to undertake some major earth-moving and recontour your land to alter its drainage patterns.

Official specifications for most sports call for the court or field to slope from side to side. When this is difficult to achieve, a court may slope from end to end or from corner to corner, but such grades tend to give an advantage to the player or team on the higher side. For large playing areas, such as football fields, the preferred slope runs from a longitudinal crown down the center of the field toward each sideline.

How steep the slope should be depends on the surface material. To drain properly, a grass playing field needs at least a 2 per cent slope—a drop of about 2½ inches for every 10 feet. Official specifications for football fields call for a slope of only 1 per cent, but that implies an elaborate network of underground drainage channels. You can build such a drainage system—and you may have to if natural drainage is extremely poor—but it is expensive and laborious. More likely you will want to compromise, and grade to a slightly steeper slope.

For paved surfaces, the generally accepted slope is about 1 per cent, usually 1 inch for every 10 feet. Underground drainage lines are neither needed nor desirable beneath a paved playing area; instead, the court is sloped to direct runoff into drainage pipes set around the court's perimeter. Porous playing surfaces like those on many tennis courts can be graded to the gentlest slope of all—0.5 per cent, about 1 inch in 20 feet. Most water seeps through the playing surface and is carried off by a base of crushed stone.

For a playing surface to maintain proper drainage pitch, the slope must first be cut into what professional excavators call the area's subgrade. This is the actual depth of the excavation, over which layers of such materials as crushed stone, stone dust and topsoil are laid. The final grade is the finished surface level of the court or playing field.

For a relatively small playing area, as for badminton or volleyball, you may be able to establish the subgrade yourself, using a string grid and reshaping the ground with garden tools. For larger areas or sites that are not close to the desired slope, you need a professional excavator. Trimming down even a gentle hillside can require shifting a huge amount of soil. For example, cutting a tennis court from a hill that slopes just 6 inches over the court's length means moving 1,800 cubic feet of soil—eight large truckloads.

Whether you do the job yourself or hire an excavator, grading is done in three basic ways: by cutting down high ground to the level of a lower area, by filling in low areas to bring them up to the level of higher ground, or by a combination of cutting and filling to eliminate both high and low areas.

Cutting down the existing grade has one important advantage over the other two: The newly exposed earth is generally very stable from years of natural compaction. A disadvantage of cutting is that large quantities of earth must be relocated on your property or hauled away at your expense. For this reason the most commonly used method is the combination of cut and fill. If you plan carefully, the volume of earth cut away will roughly balance the amount needed as fill. But a filled area must be thoroughly compacted and this is best accomplished with an excavator's heavy equipment.

For most grading jobs it is sufficient to indicate the boundaries of the area to be excavated and tell the excavator which way you want the land to slope and what you want its level to be in relation to the surrounding property. But many recreational activities have very narrow tolerances for deviations in ground level. An above-ground swimming pool, for example, must rest on ground varying no more than 2 inches around its perimeter (page 96). For a tennis court, where the tolerance is most critical, deviation in grade

from the built-in drainage slope can be no more than ⅛ inch.

To produce surfaces of this accuracy, you must draw up a precise grading plan; the best tool for this purpose is a transit level, a surveyor's instrument that excavators also use to check their work. A transit level's readings are not of actual heights—they are all relative measurements, taken in relation to an arbitrary fixed point somewhere outside the area to be graded and marked with a stake. This will be your constant point of reference throughout the grading process.

When you first set up the transit over this reference point, note the instrument's height by measuring the grade (page 18) at a benchmark on your property. This mark can be the top of a low wall or step, a sidewalk corner, or any object that will not be disturbed during your work. Set the transit at this height each time you use the instrument. If you cannot duplicate the height exactly, you must take the new height of the instrument into account when you make any new grade measurements.

The first step in developing a grading plan is to plot the four corners of your field, using the techniques shown on page 17 for establishing right angles. With a transit level, measure the difference in the existing grade at these four points and record the measurements on a rough diagram of the site. For a field crested down the middle, take readings also at the midpoints of the end lines.

Evaluate these measurements and select new measurements that will create the desired slope with the least amount of earth-moving. To get a 1 per cent slope on a 50-by-100-foot field having a transit-level reading of 50 inches along its upper sideline, for example, you will need to create a grade that measures 56 inches along the lower sideline—the higher transit reading indicating a lower grade.

Write these new measurements on your grading plan, noting the difference between them and the existing measurements; this tells you how much higher or lower the surface must be at each point. Then use the offset reference stakes shown on page 18 to guide the excavator in establishing the subgrade at the new levels you have calculated.

Grading with Garden Tools

1 Preparing the subgrade. For a small court, set the tines of a rotary tiller for shallow tilling and run the machine back and forth across the area to break up grass roots or weeds. Rake off the debris and cart it away. With a pick and shovel, loosen the soil and redistribute it until the area is roughly level, cutting down high spots and filling in low spots; use a wheelbarrow to move soil if you are changing the grade of a natural slope. Then crisscross the area again with the rotary tiller—this time with the tines set for deep tilling—until all clods are broken up and the soil can be smoothed easily with a rake. Set stakes at the four corners of the court.

2 Establishing the slope. Tie a string to one corner stake, 6 inches from the ground. While a helper checks its position at its center with a line level, stretch the string along the end line of the court to the stake at the opposite corner. Raise or lower the string according to the helper's directions until it is level. Mark the stake at that point, then move the string down the stake until the desired slope is reached. For roughly a 2 per cent slope, lower the string 2½ inches for every 10 feet. Tie the string to the stake at that point. The string now marks one end line and indicates the proper slope of the court.

To mark the upper sideline, stretch a second string between the two stakes at the upper side of the court, using a line level to position the string so it is level. Follow the same procedure to mark the lower sideline. Complete the remaining end line by tying a string between the last two unconnected stakes at the points where the sideline strings cross them.

3 Finishing the grade. Create a grid over the court by setting stakes along its boundary lines at 6-foot intervals and connecting them with strings. First connect the end-line stakes, then weave a set of cross-court strings over and under the first set, so the strings support each other. Make sure the strings are taut; if they touch the ground, remove any obstacles that cause them to lie unevenly.

Working over one 6-foot square at a time, redistribute the soil with a rake and shovel, judging by eye when each section of the court parallels the plane formed by the strings suspended above it. Make a final pass with the rake—this time with its tines facing up—to smooth the surface. When the entire court has been graded, remove all the strings and stakes and roll or tamp the area. The court is now ready for the construction of its playing surface.

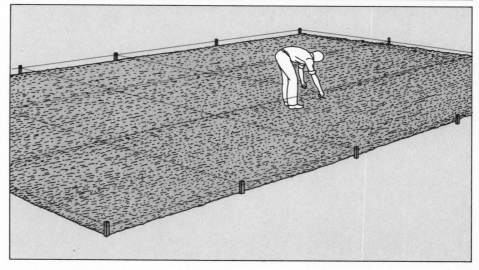

A Device to Plot Elevation Changes

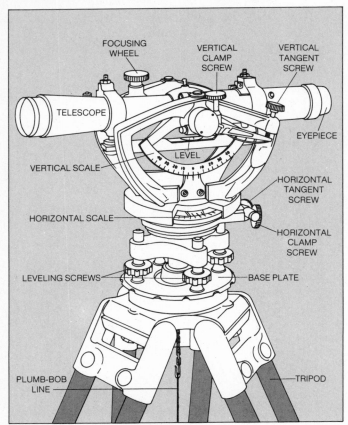

Preparing a Transit Level for Use

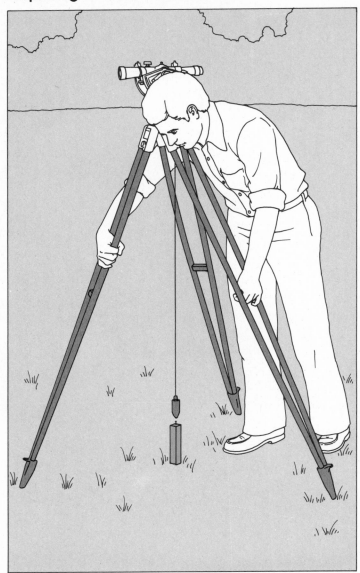

Anatomy of a transit level. For setting the perimeters of an area to be graded and comparing heights within the area, nothing is more accurate than a transit level, a surveyor's precision instrument. The heart of the transit level is its telescope; the eyepiece rotates to focus cross hairs in the scope, and the focusing wheel makes the fine adjustments.

The telescope pivots on its mounting so it can be aimed at any point on the horizon. As it moves vertically, its angle of inclination is measured on a scale that registers from 0°—the transit's level position—to 45° above or below. When moved horizontally it describes a complete circle of 360°, but the circle is broken into four 90° arcs. Once roughly on target, the telescope can be precisely aimed both horizontally and vertically by turns of the appropriate tangent screw. The two clamp screws lock the telescope in any one of its horizontal or vertical positions.

The transit is mounted on a tripod and has a plumb bob so it can be positioned directly over a specific point, such as a reference stake. The entire telescope assembly shifts slightly over the base plate to center the bob more exactly. A small spirit level is mounted under the telescope and four leveling screws on the base plate can be adjusted to level the instrument.

1 Positioning the tripod. Spread the legs of the tripod so they straddle the stake that marks the sighting position. Drive a nail into the top of the stake to provide a precise focus point. Adjust the positions of the legs, one at a time, until the plumb bob hangs within ¼ inch of the side of the nailhead. Loosen the leveling screws and shift the transit over the base plate until the bob is centered exactly over the nail, then tighten the screws again to lock the transit in place.

If you are working on a steep grade, experiment with the different angles at which the tripod legs can be set until you find a combination that keeps the transit as close to level as possible. Dig the tripod legs firmly into the ground. If the tripod on your transit level has telescoping legs, you can also adjust the length of the legs to help center the bob over the stake.

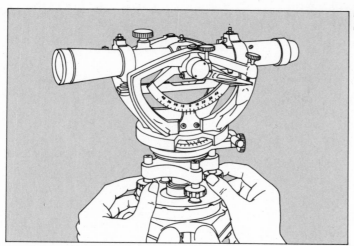

2 **Leveling the telescope.** Loosen the leveling screws slightly and rotate the telescope until it is aligned over two of the leveling screws that are opposite each other. Slowly turn those two screws in opposite directions until the bubble in the spirit level is centered. Rotate the scope 90° to align it over the other pair of screws and adjust them until the bubble is again centered in the level. Repeat this procedure several times, alternately adjusting the two pairs of screws, until the telescope remains level when it is swung around in a complete circle.

Boundary Sighting for a Court or Field

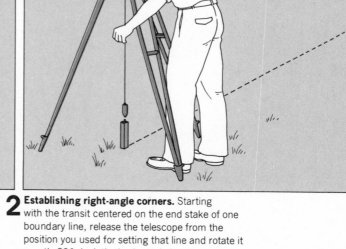

1 **Setting stakes in line.** After driving two stakes to mark the direction of one side of the field, plumb and level the transit over the stake that will mark one end of the line. Focus the vertical cross hair of the telescope on the center of the other stake and tighten the horizontal clamp screw to lock the telescope in that position.

Set other stakes along this same line by having a helper pace off the approximate position of the next stake and hold it upright at that point. Pivot the telescope up or down (but not horizontally) until you have the new stake in view. Guide the helper right or left until the center of the new stake also lines up exactly on the vertical cross hair, then have him drive the stake in at that point. To set stakes behind the transit, loosen the horizontal clamp screw, rotate the telescope 180° and repeat the same procedure.

2 **Establishing right-angle corners.** Starting with the transit centered on the end stake of one boundary line, release the telescope from the position you used for setting that line and rotate it exactly 90°; lock the horizontal clamp screw. Once again, have a helper move a stake across the instrument's field of vision until the center of the stake aligns with the vertical cross hair. Drive the stake in at that point. Continue to add stakes to establish a second boundary line. Then check to make sure the two boundary lines form a right angle by swinging the scope back 90° to its original position: It should still focus on the first line of stakes.

Establishing a Series of Reference Stakes

1 Laying out the grading area. To guide the excavator as he works, mark the area to be graded with a series of stakes: one at each corner, plus eight offset stakes—one 10 feet beyond each corner in each direction—to use in reconstructing the boundaries when the grading is complete. If the graded area is to have a center crown, add a stake at the midpoint of each end line.

To set the stakes, use the location-sighting techniques shown on page 17 and move the transit through the sequence of four positions shown in the diagrams below. The circles indicate the positions of the transit around the site. The arrows and dashed lines at each position indicate the directions in which you must sight the transit to place the stakes you need.

For the offset stakes marking the sidelines and the center crown, use 5-foot 2-by-4s, so you can write grading instructions on them that the excavator can read without leaving his machine. The other stakes can be 1-by-2s. Label each 2-by-4 offset stake with its location relative to its boundary stake: offset 10'N (10 feet north), offset 10'S (10 feet south), for example.

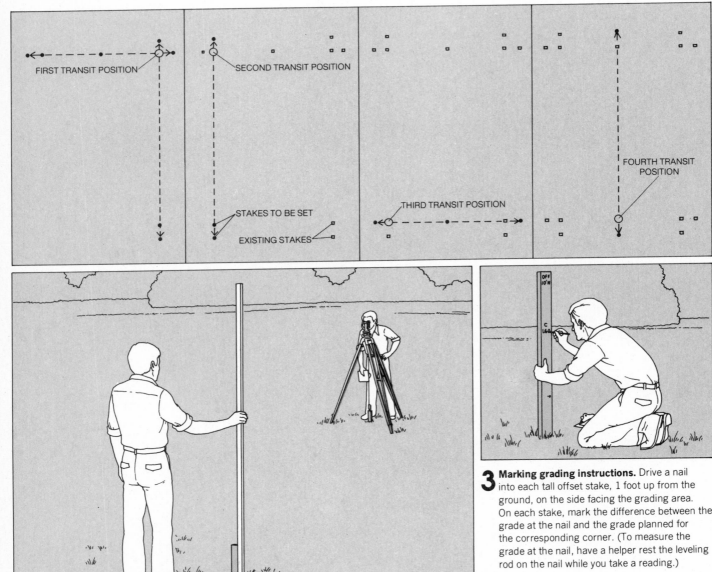

FIRST TRANSIT POSITION

SECOND TRANSIT POSITION

STAKES TO BE SET

EXISTING STAKES

THIRD TRANSIT POSITION

FOURTH TRANSIT POSITION

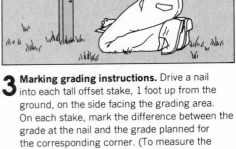

3 Marking grading instructions. Drive a nail into each tall offset stake, 1 foot up from the ground, on the side facing the grading area. On each stake, mark the difference between the grade at the nail and the grade planned for the corresponding corner. (To measure the grade at the nail, have a helper rest the leveling rod on the nail while you take a reading.)

If the existing grade at the corner is too high, mark the stake with a *C*, indicating that earth must be cut away. If the existing grade is too low, mark the stake with an *F*, for fill. Be sure to make the number and letter large enough for the excavator to read without dismounting from his machine. The excavator will cut or fill to the difference in grade you have indicated.

2 Making the grading plan. Level the transit over a reference stake set well away from the area to be graded and preferably on its low side. Lock the telescope's vertical scale at 0°, and have a helper hold a leveling rod or a 6-foot rule upright, resting on the ground at a corner stake. Focus the telescope on the rod and note the measurement at the cross hairs. Record the measurement to the nearest ⅛ inch or ¹/₁₀₀ foot, depending on which system the excavator prefers. Take readings at the other three corners. Use these measurements to formulate a grading plan, calculating how many inches must be cut or filled at each point to create the desired grade.

A Retaining Wall to Hold a Hill

When space is at a premium and you must grade into a hillside to create a level playing surface, or add landfill to build up a low area, you will need a retaining wall to hold the earth in place. It should be solidly constructed since it will have to hold back tons of earth, and it should be built with proper drainage, to carry off the water that otherwise would add to the pressure behind it.

Check the drainage ordinances and building codes in your area before beginning construction of a wall. In many localities a retaining wall and its drainage system require a special building permit, and plans for it must be drawn by a structural engineer. This is necessary because any significant change in the contour of the land is likely to affect the natural flow of water across it. The best drainage design incorporates weep holes in the base of the wall, backed up by a perforated pipe embedded in a layer of coarse gravel behind the wall.

Masonry and concrete are the most commonly used materials for the wall itself, but heavy timbers are also sufficiently strong and are generally easier to work with. Discarded railroad ties have long provided an inexpensive supply of heavy timbers for use in outdoor construction. However, in many areas they are becoming hard to find and the creosote that is used as a preservative on them is poisonous to plants.

If railroad ties are not available, redwood, cedar or pressure-treated pine or poplar timbers are good alternatives. Redwood is expensive but it is the handsomest of the four and it is naturally moisture-resistant. Lumberyards usually stock timbers in 6-by-6- or 6-by-8-inch sizes and in various lengths. The easiest length to work with is 8 feet; longer timbers may be too heavy to manipulate.

To tailor the timbers to the lengths you need, use a chain saw. If you rent the saw, be sure it has been properly maintained—its teeth should be sharp and its chain tight and well-lubricated. As you work, you will need to adjust the chain tension and keep the chain oiled—both routine procedures. For safety, mark guidelines on the timbers to indicate where you plan to cut, and check to be sure the timbers are free of nails along the cutting lines. Set a timber on sturdy supports and start the saw's engine on the ground, bracing the saw with your foot. When sawing, use both handholds; keep both hands on the saw as you work, and warn helpers to stand clear of the saw while it is in use.

The timbers, once cut, can be joined to each other with 10-inch steel spikes and 60-penny nails, both of which are available at lumberyards that carry the timbers. An alternative technique is to tie in each succeeding course of timbers with pegs cut from steel reinforcing rods, commonly called rebar. Rebar pegs are less expensive than the spikes but require an additional step: You will have to drill a hole before inserting each peg.

1 Constructing the bottom course. Dig a trench 1 foot wide for the first row of timbers, marking the position of the trench by running a string between two stakes set at the opposite ends of the retaining wall. Position the string 6 inches above the lowest point along the line, using a line level and a ruler to determine that the string's position is correct. Beginning at the low point and working toward the two end stakes, dig out behind the string to an even 6-inch depth below the string, measuring frequently to maintain this depth.

Cut timbers to fit the length of the trench, calculating the cuts so no timber will be less than 6 feet long. Drill ⅜-inch vertical holes through the timbers 6 inches from each end, using an electrician's ship-auger bit in a heavy-duty drill. Lay the timbers in the trench end to end, against the front edge of the trench.

2 Setting a tilt in the wall. Adjust the timbers in the trench so they are level from end to end, then tilt all the timbers back ¼ inch toward the uphill side. To obtain the correct tilt, prop up the front edges of the timbers with a few handfuls of gravel and, holding a level across the top of each timber, measure the gap between the bottom of the horizontal level and the back edge of the tilted timber. Add or remove gravel until the gap measures ¼ inch.

Spike the timbers to the ground by driving 42-inch lengths of ⅜-inch rebar through holes drilled near the timber ends, using a 10-pound sledge hammer. Scratch chalk lines on the faces of the timbers, marking each spike location so that in setting the next course, you can avoid these spikes. Similarly mark the spike locations on all subsequent courses.

3 Securing the second course. Lay a second course of timbers on top of the first, this time leaving 1-inch gaps between the timber ends, as weep holes; stagger the timbers so the gaps do not fall directly over the joints of the bottom course. Using a 10-pound sledge, drive three 10-inch steel spikes through each timber to secure it to the course below. Position the spikes at least an inch to one side of each chalk mark on the timbers below, and once again mark the position of every new spike with a chalk line.

On the uphill side of the wall, provide additional support by toenailing the two courses together every 2 feet or so with 60-penny nails.

4 Anchoring the wall to the hillside. At both ends of the wall and at 12-foot intervals in between, lay 4-foot-long deadman timbers on top of the second course, running perpendicularly back into the hillside. Dig trenches into the slope to set these deadman timbers level. At the rear of each deadman trench, dig a perpendicular trench 2 feet long and 6 inches deeper than the deadman trench. Sink a 2-foot-long timber into each of these cross trenches to serve as an anchor, or cross plate. Set the deadmen in place, flush with the front edge of the wall, and secure them to the cross plates and the wall with two 10-inch spikes at each end.

Add the third course of timbers, filling gaps between deadmen. On this course and all subsequent ones, butt the timber ends tightly together.

5 **Installing the drainage pipe.** When the third course of timbers is in, tack galvanized screening over the backs of the weep holes, spread a 6-inch-deep bed of gravel along the back of the wall and lay 4-inch perforated plastic drainage pipe on it, snaking the pipe under the deadmen, from one end of the wall to the other. Bury the pipe with another 6 inches of gravel.

Fill in behind the wall with a 4-inch layer of earth and tamp it in place, packing the earth firmly around the cross plates and deadmen. Pack in additional earth until it comes almost to the top of the third course of timbers.

6 **Completing the wall.** Construct the fourth course as you did the previous three, but anchor its end timbers to the two end deadmen by driving spikes through them. At the ends of the wall, run timbers back into the hillside at each course; these are stacked on top of the end deadmen but, unlike the deadmen, are not anchored to perpendicular cross plates. Alternate the placement of these side timbers so that one begins flush with the face of the front wall and the next one butts into the rear of the wall. Stagger the placement of the spikes to avoid hitting spikes in the course below, and fill in behind each course as it is completed. For each course, use chalk marks on the face of the wall to indicate spike locations.

When you reach the sixth course of timbers, add a second series of deadmen and cross plates, this time using 8-foot-long deadmen. Stagger the position of these deadmen so they fall midway between the first deadmen, and thoroughly tamp the backfill to anchor them in place.

Continue in this fashion to the top of the wall, using 8-foot-long deadmen to anchor every third course. Gently slope the surface of the backfill away from the wall to provide surface drainage.

Fast Drainage to Keep Your Play Area Dry

Inseparable from any grading project is planning for drainage—runoff from rainfall can be a threat to any outdoor recreational facility. Accumulations of water below the ground can buoy a swimming pool up in its hole, and water coursing across a playing field will eventually scar even the toughest surface.

Simply stated, drainage planning involves determining where water will be coming from, where it can be disposed of, and how to take it there. But several considerations will combine to dictate the kind of drainage plan needed.

One factor, of course, is the volume of water you are likely to have to deal with. The average annual rainfall and the density of land use in your neighborhood are both good indicators of what that volume will be. In heavily developed areas, as much as 95 per cent of rainfall turns into surface runoff—a tennis court in a built-up suburb, surrounded by streets and houses, will need a more elaborate drainage system than that needed by a court in an open field.

The size and shape of the land upslope from your site will also influence how much water drains into it. Remembering that water flows downhill, you should be able to discern the pattern of that runoff simply by picking out the high spots, valleys and swales. But the rate of runoff will be affected by the composition of the soil and the thickness of the vegetation on top of it. If the soil is sandy, much of the water is likely to seep into the ground before it ever reaches your court, and a thick ground cover will slow the rate at which the runoff moves.

You will also have alternatives in disposing of the water. The simplest method is to channel the water so that it flows in a controlled pattern over the surface of the ground to a point below your playing field. But you must be careful not to channel it toward your house or into a neighbor's yard. Lacking an adequate low point, you may have to construct a dry well—a large rock-filled hole into which excess water can drain—or run the water into an existing storm sewer; either of

these solutions requires permission from local authorities.

In some cases a surface drainage system can involve nothing more than sloping the area surrounding your site to carry rainfall away, much as you slope the playing surface itself. On other sites you may have to intercept the water by cutting shallow drainage paths, known as swales, uphill from the site and at an angle to the flow of water. Swales are a routine landscaping device.

Where drainage is particularly bad, and soil holds water for a long time, you may have to go underground for your solution and construct one of the subsoil drainage systems shown opposite. In a subsoil system, water is collected in perforated pipes embedded in gravel-filled trenches, and is transported by the force of gravity to a point below the site. The pipes can be of plastic, concrete or clay, but plastic pipe is least expensive and is the easiest to use. For the system to carry off the water effectively, the pipes must slope at least 1 inch in every 20 feet.

A system of swales and berms. In this plan for a surface drainage system to carry off water from newly leveled ground around a swimming pool, a swale is cut uphill from the pool and links with an existing swale, which was made when the house was built. To create a swale, remove soil to a depth of 6 to 10 inches in a swath 2 to 3 feet wide, and use the soil from the swale to construct a lip of earth, which is called a berm, on the downhill side. Line the swale with a 3-inch layer of gravel, then add topsoil and seed the entire swale, top and sides, with grass.

Perimeter drainage. This simple underground drainage design, surrounding a court on four sides, serves two purposes: It collects and disposes of water that drains off the playing surface, and it intercepts the underground seepage of water from points outside the court area, a function that makes it particularly valuable for courts built in low-lying areas. In this system, perforated pipes are laid in trenches 24 to 30 inches deep several feet beyond the court, and are surrounded by at least 4 inches of coarse crushed stone or coarse gravel. The gravel can fill the drainage trenches right to the top or can stop short of the top and be covered with a layer of sandy topsoil planted with a ground cover.

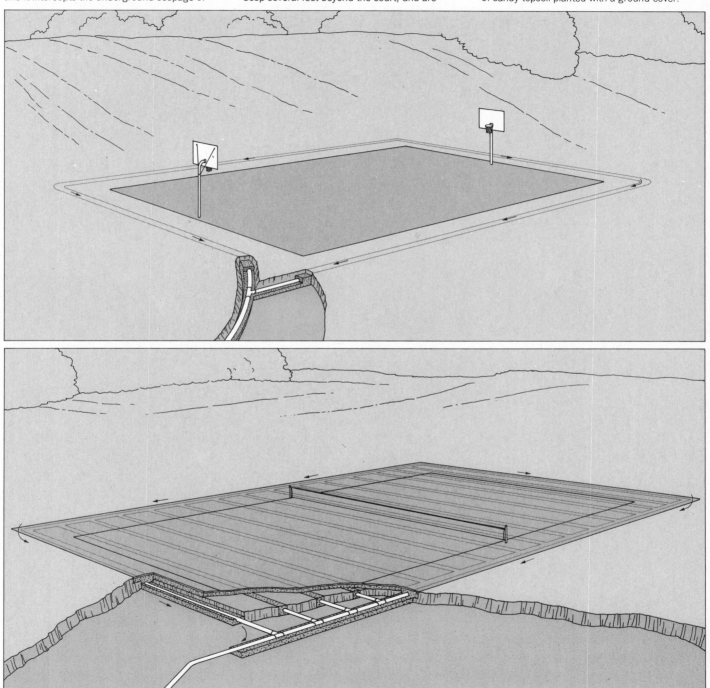

Full-field drainage. This elaborate underground drainage system, necessary only in areas where natural drainage is extremely poor, is normally installed only beneath a porous playing surface. The perforated pipes are set in gravel-filled trenches approximately 30 inches beneath the ground, underlying the crushed-stone base of the playing surface. As shown here, the system has a double pitch, with cross-field drainage lines sloping toward the lower side of the court and with perimeter collector lines pitched toward an outflow at the lower left side of the drawing.

2 Play Surfaces Suited to the Game

A liner for setting limits. Most outdoor games are played within a fixed area determined by boundary lines and crisscrossed with a grid of base lines, service lines, center lines, net lines, spiking lines, goal lines or penalty lines. This field-marking machine with its funnel-like hopper is used to mark grass, clay and other porous playing surfaces. Rolling along a string guideline, it drops marking powder through a line-wide slot when a trigger on the handle is pulled.

More than any soccer shoe or baseball glove, a playing surface can decide a game's outcome. This is obvious in a game such as golf, where the object is literally to overcome the irregularities of the course. In almost all other games, this element of surprise is supplied by the player's opponent, while the playing surface itself is supposed to be uniform, predictable and, typically, flat. Yet everyone who has ever been defeated by a bad bounce on a field or court knows that not all surfaces are created equal.

Building the desired uniformity into a playing surface used to be a simple matter of accurately grading the site and covering it with a standard surfacing material such as grass or asphalt. Although grading is as important as ever, today for a price you can choose from a wealth of surfaces, many of them equal to the best professional ones. Among them are acrylic texture coatings, asphaltic emulsions that cushion your feet, fast-drying greenstone and removable plastic mats. Today even grass surfaces have become scientific—certain kinds of turf let a ball roll faster than others.

Some playing surfaces are expensive to install; others are relatively economical. A man-made ice-skating rink may cost only as much as the water needed to flood an area of lawn. In most cases the costs are discretionary, since many games can be played on whatever surface is available—grass, dirt, the natural ice of a pond. By sacrificing durability or drainage—leaving out some of the layers of crushed rock beneath a putting green, settling for a thinner layer of asphalt on a basketball court—you can easily reduce your costs. In fact, this is probably wise if the play area or field is intended for youngsters who will be leaving home in a few years.

However, other features of a field or court, most often the size and shape, cannot be so easily altered—and for good reason. Like rumors, games tend to spawn variations of themselves so easily that no single version can survive long unless its rules—including some minimal specifications for the playing surface—are codified by some universally recognized group such as a sports association. For example, what we call tennis began as a kind of handball played by the ancient Greeks outdoors in courtyards. During the Renaissance it was played indoors with parchment-covered racquets in a narrow, walled court with a winglike net. Tennis was reborn as an outdoor game in England in the 1870s when a Major Wingfield invented a version for croquet courts. Soon thereafter the croquet club at Wimbledon changed tennis radically for the last time and ended the chaos by regulating court dimensions and rules. But tennis keeps breeding related games—paddle tennis, platform tennis, table tennis, each requiring its own regulation playing surface.

Natural Advantages of Grass: Tough, Soft, Springy

Grass was the original playing surface for many outdoor games and remains a favorite today. Whether backyard lawn for neighborhood softball or manicured turf for golf putting green, any grass playing field offers advantages. Softer and springier than any paved surface, it is easier on players' legs and makes for gentler landings. In golf and lawn tennis, its texture adds a natural element to the play that no man-made surface can supply.

Like any playing surface, a grass lawn should be fairly level and have good natural drainage or a supplementary tile or pipe drainage system so that the area dries quickly. In addition, it needs a porous layer of topsoil, and a variety of grass that can withstand heavy wear. In northern regions, the hardiest turf grasses are a blend of at least three Kentucky bluegrasses, or they are turf-type perennial rye grass or a tall fescue such as Kentucky-31. In warm areas, grasses such as Bermuda grass, Zoysia, and Bahia are used on most athletic fields.

Before installing a new grass playing field or converting an existing lawn to this purpose, test the soil to determine whether lime or other nutrients should be added. For a new lawn, till the soil to a depth of 6 inches, adding sand, decomposed peat and fertilizer to ensure a good start. Ideally, the topsoil should include 50 to 75 per cent sand and 10 to 15 per cent decomposed peat or other organic matter. Rake the area smooth, breaking up any large clumps of soil and removing debris, and soak the ground well before planting the grass, whatever its form— seed, sprigs or sod. Thereafter maintain the lawn according to the following procedures, which will improve the turf's quality and help it withstand heavy wear.

Aerating—letting air into the soil— once or twice a year helps alleviate soil compaction, caused by the repeated pounding of players' feet. Compacted soil keeps air and water from reaching grass roots and results in worn, thin turf.

For most effective aeration, use a power-driven spoon-type aerator, which can be rented from many garden-supply or lawn-equipment stores. The hollow tines of this aerator perforate the lawn, pulling out tiny plugs of turf and soil 3 to 4 inches long, letting water and fertilizer penetrate deep into the soil. The best time to aerate depends on the particular grass and its growing season, but early autumn and very early spring are usually best. Be sure there are at least three weeks of growing weather after you aerate, to give the grass time to recover.

Occasionally it may be necessary to cut away thatch—the heavy accumulation of dead grass that sometimes forms on the surface of the soil, creating a dense mat that deprives roots of water and nutrients and provides a breeding ground for insects and disease. A power-driven dethatcher with vertical blades is the best way to remove thatch without damaging the grass roots. Ordinarily, dethatching is needed only when thatch accumulates to more than half an inch.

As with any lawn, a grass playing field should be watered regularly and fertilized in the spring and early fall. Timing will vary with the region and type of grass, but in any case always fertilize after aerating or dethatching, when nutrients have best access to the soil. The schedule for weed control will vary, too, but preemergent crabgrass killers should be applied in early spring and broad-leaf weed killers in the spring or fall, as needed.

To keep playing-field turf at its prime, mow it slightly higher than you would an ornamental lawn. Bermuda grass and Zoysia are best kept ½ to 1 inch high; Kentucky bluegrass, tall fescues and rye grass should be cut 1½ to 2 inches high. If you shorten tall grass, do so gradually; grass is weakened if it loses more than one third of its height at one time.

Even with the best care, athletic-field turf is bound to develop worn spots at the points of heaviest play—near the net line in a volleyball court, for instance, or down the center of a touch-football field. If the worn spot is low as well as bald, dig in extra topsoil so the spot is about an inch higher than the surrounding area; when it settles, it will become level with the rest of the field. Then repair the area by reseeding it or patching it with sod lifted from other areas of the yard.

In addition to keeping the turf in good condition, you will need to mark boundaries on it. For an occasional game of touch football or badminton, it is probably sufficient to mark the four corners of the field with *ad hoc* markers of some sort—plastic bottles filled with sand or water, bean bags, or conical "witch hats" like those used as traffic markers. Schools and athletic teams commonly use foam-rubber pylons, which you can make yourself or buy at sporting-goods stores.

To mark lines on the grass, you can use either water-based latex paint or a dry powdered material. Painted lines may last several weeks even in rainy weather; powdered lines give you more flexibility because they can be hosed away quickly. Both the latex paint and the equipment for spraying it are more expensive than the materials for powdered lines. A hand-pumped paint-spraying machine costs about as much as an inexpensive power lawn mower, while a machine for marking dry lines costs about one quarter that amount. Although paint-spraying machines cannot be rented easily, you may be able to borrow one from a school or athletic club. Or you can simply paint the lines with a narrow paint roller.

The device used to lay dry lines is frequently referred to as a limer because agricultural lime (or hydrated or granular lime) was commonly used to mark athletic fields until it was found to be caustic to eyes, clothing and skin. If you use a limer, fill it with a noncaustic powder— sand, pulverized shells or special field-marking powder available at sports or garden-supply stores. You can also mark lines by shaking the marking powder out of a coffee can, using boards as templates to create straight edges.

Whether you use paint or powder, the procedures for establishing the boundaries are the same. First stake out one of the two sidelines for the court (refer to the appendix on regulation court sizes, pages 130-133); then establish two right-angle corners, and measure off the two end lines and the other sideline, staking them as well. Run strings between the stakes as guidelines, then trace over them with your sprayer or limer. Establish guidelines for circles or semicircles by using a string compass and a small trail of marking powder. Trace these too, and then remove all nails and strings. Leave the stakes in place, driven flush with the soil surface, to serve as reference points for retracing the lines when they fade.

Rejuvenating Tired Turf

Aerating a compacted lawn. Soak the soil thoroughly to soften it, then run the aerator across the area three to five times, in alternating directions. Walk at a slow, even pace; if you move too fast, the machine will tear at the surface of the turf instead of pulling out clean plugs. After aerating, let the plugs dry on the ground until they are crumbly, then drag a flexible metal mat or a section of chain link fencing across the lawn to break them up. Spread on a top dressing of sand or a mixture of sand and decomposed peat; rake that and the broken cores over the lawn to fill in the holes. Fertilize and water well.

Overseeding a thin area. Loosen the top ½ inch of soil by chopping gently up and down with a spade, working in a crosshatched pattern but taking care not to uproot the remaining grass. Sprinkle the area with grass seed; keep it moist until the new grass is 2 to 3 inches high.

Removing thatch. With the blades of the dethatcher set to fall about ⅛ inch above the level of the ground—they should cut into the thatch but not into the ground—run the dethatcher back and forth across the lawn as you would a lawn mower, working in slightly overlapping, parallel rows. If the dethatcher is not equipped with a catcher, rake the loose thatch off the lawn.

Reseeding a bare spot. Prepare the soil as you would for a new lawn, scattering grass seed and settling it into the soil by lightly dragging a leaf rake, upside down, over the area. Water daily, keeping the soil moist until the new grass is 2 to 3 inches high. If the weather is very hot or windy, mulch with a thin layer of straw to keep the soil moist and the seeds in place.

Laying a Field in a Hurry

1 Unrolling the sod. Roll out the strips of sod over the prepared soil, butting the edges tightly together. The sod should be evenly cut and no more than ½ to ¾ inch thick. Arrange the strips as you would bricks, staggering the ends. To keep the prepared soil smooth and undisturbed, work across the area from the side on which the sod has already been laid. Protect the sod from shifting under your weight by kneeling on pieces of plywood or heavy corrugated cardboard. Using two boards, work your way across the area in steppingstone fashion.

2 Filling the seams. Fill any visible gaps between strips of sod with a damp mixture of decomposed peat moss and fertilizer and press down firmly. As the sod establishes itself, grass will grow to fill the seams, usually in a few weeks.

3 Tamping the sod. Press down lightly on the surface of the sod with a tamping tool or roller to eliminate air pockets and to put the roots in contact with the soil. Encourage the roots to knit into the soil by keeping the area moist, watering it several times a day if necessary, and leaving the area undisturbed for at least two weeks.

Boundaries Square and True

1 Staking out a sideline. Stretch a string between nails driven into the tops of two stakes that mark the correct distance for the sideline of your field. The stakes should be driven into the ground until their tops are at ground level.

2 Creating an end line. With the aid of two helpers and two steel measuring tapes, plot a right-angle triangle at one end of the sideline. Measure off 3 feet from the sideline stake (A) and drive in a reference stake (B), hammering a nail into its top. Have one helper hook a steel tape over stake A and hold the tape at the 4-foot mark, while the second helper hooks the second tape over stake B and holds that tape at the 5-foot mark. Have the helpers swing their tapes until the 4-foot and 5-foot marks intersect; mark this point (C) with a third reference stake. Use stake A and stake C to establish the position of the end line, then measure off the correct length and mark the line with stake and string.

Follow the same technique to make right angles at the other corners and establish the other sideline and the other end line. Check your work by comparing the two diagonal measurements of the field, which should be identical. Measure and mark other straight lines in the same fashion.

For large courts or fields, use larger triangles whose sides are multiples of 3, 4 and 5; for example, 6-8-10, 9-12-15 or 15-20-25.

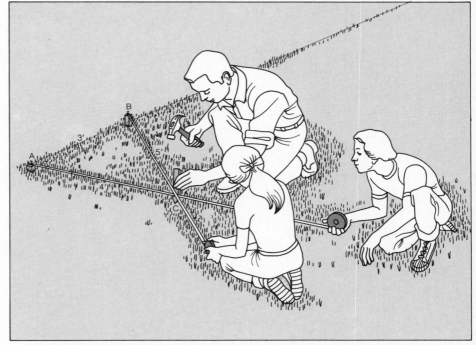

3 Completing the field markings. To plot guidelines for circular or semicircular field markings, drive a stake and nail at the circle's center point and cut a piece of string the length of the radius of the circle. Tie one end of the string around the nail and the other around the nozzle of a squeeze bottle that you have filled with marking powder or chalk. Swing the bottle in an arc along the ground, keeping the string taut, while you squeeze out a small line of powder.

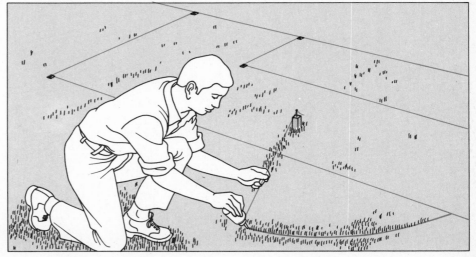

Marking Lines with Powder or Paint

Lining with marking powder. If you are using a limer *(below, left)*, fill it with marking powder and center the slot at the bottom of the bin *(inset)* directly over a string guideline at one end of the field. Pull the trigger on the handle to open the slot and trace the guidelines on the field. To make sharp corners, close the slot when you reach the end of a line and position the machine over the next line before reopening the slot.

To make straight lines without a limer, shake the marking material out of a 1-pound coffee can with a slot 1 inch long and ⅜ inch wide cut in the plastic lid *(below, right)*. Tape the lid to the can to hold it firm. Lay two parallel 2-by-4s on opposite sides of the string guideline, setting the distance between them to the desired line width; the longer the boards, the quicker the job will go. Hold the can at least a foot above the ground

and shake it gently to dust the area between the boards. Reposition the same pair of boards along the string as you work.

At corners, make a sharp angle by butting a third, short board across the ends of the long boards. Spread a piece of paper nearby as you work so that you can brush excess powder off the boards when it piles up too high.

Lining with paint. Using a 3-inch-wide paint roller, mark lines on the playing field with a mixture of 2 parts white interior latex paint to 1 part water. To ensure that the lines will be straight, be careful to align the handle of the roller with the string or chalk guideline. Because this paint mixture is quite thin and tends to dribble from the roller, position the bucket or other container so it is as close as possible to the line while you are painting.

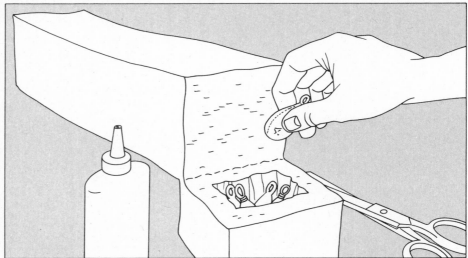

Making a flexible pylon marker. Using a pair of scissors with pointed blades, cut almost all the way across an 18-inch-high, 4-inch-square column of high-density foam rubber, 2 or 3 inches above its base. Leave one edge uncut to serve as a hinge. Snip out a hole in the base of the pylon that will be large enough to accommodate approximately 2 pounds of lead weights; leave at least an inch of foam rubber surrounding the hole so the edges of the weights will be well pad-

ded. For weights, use fishing-line sinkers, scuba divers' weights, wheel-balancing weights, small lead balls or buckshot. Nestle the weights into the hole so they are level with its top, then glue the cut edges of the pylon back together with a waterproof adhesive designed for rubber. Hold the edges together with masking tape until the glue sets. Then remove the tape and spray the pylon with fluorescent orange or red paint, or sew a bright vinyl sleeve to cover it.

Putting Greens: The Ultimate Grass Surface

Golf-course putting greens are the Rolls-Royces of athletic turfs: An extraordinary amount of both care and expense goes into their construction and maintenance.

Built to the specifications of the United States Golf Association, a putting green begins 2 feet below the surface. Four-inch drainage pipes are set in a gravel-filled trench; above this is a 4-inch layer of gravel, which is followed by a 2-inch layer of coarse sand, then a foot-deep layer of topsoil containing ingredients that have been custom-mixed according to a laboratory-prescribed formula. On top of this is planted a low, spreading type of grass, usually creeping bent grass in Northern areas and hybrid Bermuda grass in the South.

Once the grass is established, an elaborate maintenance regimen begins: mowing at least four times a week with a special multibladed greens mower to keep the grass ⅛ to ¼ inch high; watering conscientiously, often by hand, to keep the moisture content high enough to prevent the grass from wilting but low enough to prevent fungi; fertilizing once or twice a month and top-dressing the green with a fine layer of sand and topsoil several times a year; aerating twice a year; moving the hole cup at least once a week to prevent uneven wear of the turf; and protecting the grasses, which are disease-prone, by applying pesticides regularly.

Beyond all of this, stagnant dew must be knocked off the blades every morning by a spray of fresh water or by a hose or pole dragged over its surface.

Because of the expense, time and special equipment needed to build and maintain a first-class putting green, most contractors will discourage even an avid, wealthy golfer from trying to install one. In addition to the initial cost of the green, which includes the elaborate drainage system and the special soil, a new greens mower costs well over $1,000, and the yearly bill for pesticides and fertilizers is high. Some products, such as the powerful fungicides needed to protect bent grass, can be applied only by a licensed worker trained in their use. The deciding factor, however, is more often time than money—the daily watering and mowing are more trouble than most people want.

If you simply want the fun of putting at home and are not dismayed by a green that falls short of golf-course quality, you may want to consider one of the following compromises:

□ If your yard has good natural drainage, it is possible to forgo the elaborate layers of pipe, gravel and sand, and simply plant the grass on a sandy, porous topsoil at least 6 inches deep. A healthy green can be maintained on such a surface if it is not overwatered and if fungicides and insecticides are used on a regular basis. A special greens mower still will be required to keep the grass trimmed very low, but this expense can be minimized if you can purchase a used mower from a golf course or equipment store.

□ Another way to cut costs is to plant Zoysia grass instead of Bermuda or bent grass. Zoysia is slow to establish itself—it takes as long as two years when started from plugs—but it is inexpensive and grows well in shade, and it is less susceptible to disease than the other greens grasses, which means lower maintenance costs. Zoysia grows only in warm climates; one drawback is that, like Bermuda grass, it is dormant in winter, so the green will be brown several months of the year unless it is dyed or overseeded each fall with annual rye grass. Zoysia also cannot be cut shorter than ¼ inch and has a more uneven surface than Bermuda or bent grass, giving a golf ball a slightly slower roll.

□ If you have enough space, you may opt for another type of home golf: chip shots. Since they are typically fairly short and used for lifting the ball over obstacles, chip shots can be practiced on any type of lawn. Lay out a course using the lawn's natural obstacles—flower beds, rock gardens, hedges—and vary the distances from tee to cup up to a maximum of 20 yards. Using an ordinary mower, create a small putting area for each cup by mowing the grass in a 3-foot radius around it as short as possible. Be sure to leave plenty of open space around the course, or provide a barrier—such as a tall fence or a line of trees—between the course and your house or your neighbors', to prevent injuries and broken windows.

□ Another way to set up a golf green in your yard is to cover a paved terrace with indoor/outdoor carpeting. This forms the basis for a miniature golf course. For cups on a carpeted green, it is simplest to use the portable putting disks designed for indoor use and available at most golf-equipment stores. This arrangement may meet your needs and can provide fun for children as well as adults, particularly if you build obstacles to make it more challenging.

Accessories for a grass golf green, such as a cup, cup changer and flag, may be bought used from a golf course or new through the club pro shop.

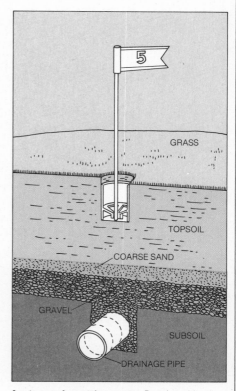

Anatomy of a putting green. Developed by the Greens Section of the United States Golf Association, these specifications for an underground drainage system as well as complex standards for mixing a proper topsoil are used in constructing putting greens on most professional golf courses. The average size of a golf-course green is 6,000 square feet.

Constructing a Base for a Good Tennis Court

If you are a serious tennis player, the idea of owning your own backyard court might not be an outrageous fantasy. Indeed, although the logistics of building a tennis court are staggering, the job is not exorbitantly expensive: On good soil the grandest court can be built for the cost of an addition to a house—with a lot of help from future tennis partners.

The first step in planning a court is determining whether your land is suitable. A full-sized tennis court covers an overall area, including nonplaying margins, of 7,200 square feet, measuring 120 feet north to south and 60 feet east to west. If your yard is slightly too small, you can opt instead for a paddle-tennis court, only 40 feet by 80 feet, but built the same way. Few options are open, however, in the court's orientation; in a badly placed court the sun will shine in one player's eyes. You will also need a fence, and in most localities there are codes dictating the minimum distance of any structure from a property line. And some communities limit the height of a fence to 6 feet—so you may need a variance to build a standard tennis-court fence, which is 10 feet high.

A tennis court consists of a graded subsurface topped with a base layer of clay or stone drainage material and a final playing surface. Naturally the condition of the land itself—its slope, drainage and soil type—will affect the cost of the court. You can, if you like, consult a local agricultural extension agent or soil engineer before proceeding. Generally, however, if your soil is relatively porous and your yard is flat, high above the water table and full of clay, you can probably avoid the expense of a special drainage system (pages 22-23) to keep the court dry, or a retaining wall (pages 19-21) to maintain the court's level surface.

Laying out, clearing and grading the court site to the demanding tolerances required for tennis is a painstaking task calling for the continual use of a transit level and leveling rod (pages 16-18) plus the help of a careful contractor with a bulldozer. The earth should be graded to within 2 inches of the desired grade level, and the whole court must slope slightly from one side to the other to let water run off. On nonporous courts—asphalt and concrete—this slope should be 6 inches; porous ones of dirt and clay need to slope only 3 inches because some water sinks into them.

During the grading, all vegetation must be removed from the area. Trees must not only be cut down—their entire root systems must be dug out. Also, the whole site must be treated with a herbicide to prevent anything from growing back later to spoil the court surface.

The type of drainage layer you build depends on what the finished playing surface will be and is one of the biggest factors in the cost of the court. Dirt and clay courts, although not cheap, are usually built without the expensive crushed-stone drainage layers shown on the following pages. You must, however, grade the site, install a brick curb to hold the surfacing material in place, and then sift back onto it 100 tons of soil—in many cases, dug up from the court itself by the bulldozer operator.

The soil is sifted through ¼-inch screen mesh stretched over 4-by-8-foot wooden frames, and is spread and leveled. You might be able to play on this surface. More likely the soil will prove to be very slow-drying—most clay and dirt courts are—and the surface will benefit from a dusting of a special fast-drying court-surfacing material (page 38).

To build an all-clay court, you must have the right type of clay. Your local agricultural extension agent should be able to tell you whether your soil is suitable. To test the soil for clay content yourself, dig up about a cup of it, let it dry and then break it into granules. Mix 3 tablespoons of water into it, mold it with your hands into a cake 1 inch thick, then let it dry. If your soil contains the right amount of clay for a tennis court, this cake will not be crumbly when it dries.

For a more durable court, especially on poorly drained land, it is advisable—even on clay courts—to install two base layers of crushed stone (pages 36-37). The first should be of coarsely crushed, ¾-inch stone, the second should be a leveling layer of fine stone dust.

The large amounts of these materials you will need to blanket a full-sized court site to a depth of 4 inches—approximately 165 tons of coarse stone and 20 tons of stone dust—will have to be trucked in directly from a quarry. Explain at the quarry that you will need the assistance of the driver who delivers the coarse stone—he must empty it evenly over the court into rows. The stone dust can simply be dumped at the edge of the court; you can then wheelbarrow it onto the court yourself. Once this layer of stone dust is smoothed to the exacting specifications required—with no point on the court more than ⅛ inch off—the court is ready for its final surfacing.

One option you may consider before building the base for a porous court is a sprinkler system to keep the surface moist. A porous court must be wetted down constantly—as often as it becomes dusty—but you can eliminate much of this drudgery by installing a system consisting of 1¼-inch plastic pipes feeding two sprinkler heads at opposite sides of the court. If you want to run the pipes under the court itself, you will have to lay them just before installing the stone base, but you can just as easily add the sprinkler system after the court is finished by running the pipes around the perimeter of the court.

An asphalt court, in some ways the easiest of all courts to build, requires the same base of crushed stone, but needs of course no sprinkler system. Nor does it need a brick curb around the perimeter to hold the asphalt in place—the contractor who installs the asphalt can bank the edges and tamp them to form a beveled end around the stone base.

Orienting the Court and Establishing Its Borders

1 Orienting the court. Set a 1-by-2 stake at a point chosen for one corner of the court and the direction of one side by sighting and staking another point 60 feet away with a transit level (*pages 16-18*). Extend this line another 60 feet by sighting past this stake with the transit level, to establish the opposite corner of the court.

If you live north of the 38th parallel—the approximate latitude of San Francisco, Wichita and Richmond—the court should run as nearly true north-south as possible; farther south, its axis should be shifted 22° toward north-northwest so that the sun will not blind either player in fall and winter. Consult your local building inspector's office to find out the discrepancy in your locale between magnetic north—indicated by a compass—and true north.

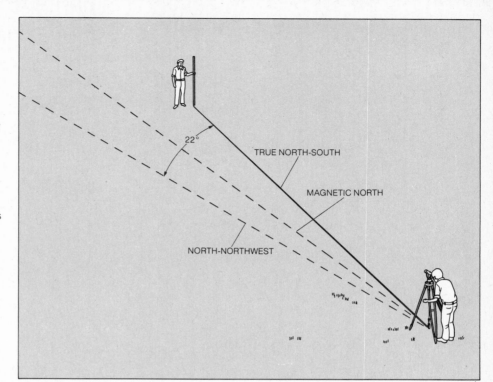

22°
TRUE NORTH-SOUTH
MAGNETIC NORTH
NORTH-NORTHWEST

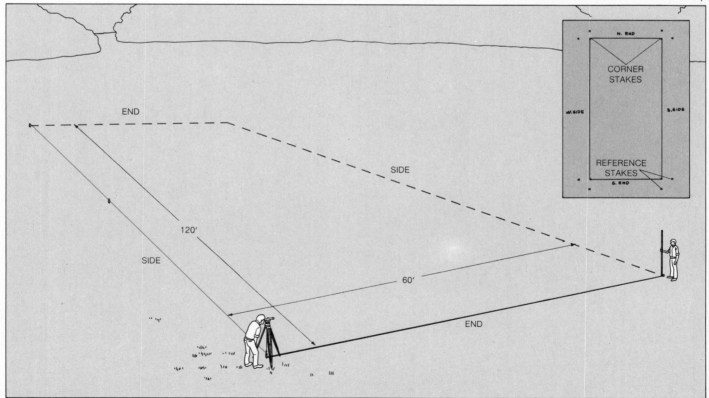

END
SIDE
120'
SIDE
60'
END

CORNER STAKES
REFERENCE STAKES
N. END
W. SIDE
E. SIDE
S. END

2 Staking the corners. With the transit level still in the same position, sight along the side of the court and set reference stakes 10 feet beyond both ends of it (*inset*) to use in reconstructing the court boundaries when grading is complete.

Locate the end of the court by turning the transit level 90° and sighting to set a corner stake 60 feet away, at the same time setting reference stakes 10 feet beyond this line at both ends. Move the transit level to the newly established corner stake, locate and stake the other side of the court and set reference stakes as before. Finally, move the transit level to the far end of this second side and sight along the other end line of the court to set two final reference stakes.

Correcting Irregularities
in the Contour of the Site

1 **Setting up a surveying grid.** Tie strings between the corner stakes and between the reference stakes at the ends and sides of the court, and set grid stakes at 10-foot intervals along the outside strings. Number the grid stakes along each side from 1 to 13, starting with a reference stake, and letter the grid stakes along the ends from A to G. On a large piece of paper make a grid chart with corresponding labels (*inset*), noting the differences in heights needed at the lettered stakes in order to produce the proper amount of slope from side to side. For a porous court surface, the increment between stakes is ½ inch; for a nonporous surface, 1 inch.

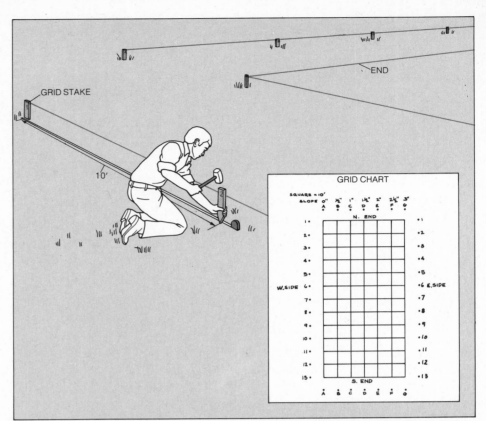

2 **Plotting the ground's contour.** From a sighting point off the court, preferably on the low side, and with a helper holding a leveling rod at each of the 91 grid points in succession, sight through the transit level to measure the height of the rod above the ground. At each corresponding grid point on the chart, note the reading.

Allowing for the fact that the site must be graded about 5 inches lower than the finished level of a porous court—7 inches lower for an asphalt court—calculate the difference between the actual reading at each grid point and its reading when properly graded. Take into account the desired side-to-side slope. The differences

indicate the amount of soil to be removed or added at each point on the grid. For example, if grid point A-1 is already at the desired graded level, and reads 50 inches, while B-3 reads 40 inches, then 10 inches of soil must be removed at B-3, plus the increment needed for the drainage slope at that particular point.

3 Filling in low areas. In low areas, where the ground falls more than 2 feet below the desired grade level, fill the depression to 1 foot below that level with 1½-inch stone. (Do not use loose soil because it may settle later.) Have the bulldozer operator compact the stones by running over them with the bulldozer treads; then top off the depression with two layers of soil, watering and compacting each layer separately.

Remove the corner stakes and have the bulldozer operator grade the entire site—plus a 2-foot margin all around the edge—to within 2 inches of the desired grade level. Check the site's contours again and rake imperfections to within ½ inch of the desired level. Compact the soil by rolling and cross-rolling a 1,000-pound roller over the entire site. Install retaining walls and drainage ditches as necessary.

A Brick Curb Designed to Contain the Surface

1 Laying a foundation. Set strings between the reference stakes ½ inch below the level desired for the final court surface. Shovel a wedge-shaped bed of ¾-inch stone around three sides of the site just inside the boundary string, tapering the bed from about 6 inches wide at the bottom to 4 inches wide at the top, and making it at least 1 inch deep—deep enough to bring the top of the bed to about 3 inches below the level desired for the finished court surface. Leave one end of the court temporarily uncurbed so dump trucks can later distribute crushed stone for the court's base more easily. If you intend to install fence posts within the curb, leave 2-foot gaps in the gravel bed every 8 feet.

2 Leveling the curb. Atop the bed of stone, lay a single layer of bricks on a bed of mortar deep enough to bring the outside edge of the bricks level with the strings set between the reference stakes. Adjust the depth of the mortar bed as necessary and bank the sides of the bricks with mortar too (inset), but do not put mortar between the ends of the bricks.

MORTAR

4½"

GRAVEL BED

Laying a Crushed-Stone Base to Speed Drainage

1 Setting grade stakes. Hammer a line of stakes along all the lettered grid rows, setting the stakes 6 feet apart; set a matching row of stakes along both 120-foot sides of the court, 1 foot in from the brick curb. While a helper checks the height of each stake with a transit level, use a leveling rod to set the top of each stake ½ inch below the level of the bricks. Nail 1-by-4 horizontal strips to the first two rows of stakes along one side, flush with the tops of the stakes; these strips will serve as guides in screeding, that is, leveling, the crushed stone.

Have the driver of the dump truck delivering ¾-inch crushed stone back the truck into the open (curbless) end of the court and steer his truck between the two screed strips, to the opposite end. Then, as the truck bed rises, the truck should move forward, depositing the stone as evenly as possible to a level just slightly above the screed strips. (When all the crushed stone has been delivered, complete the brick curb across the open end of the court.)

SCREED STRIP

GRADE STAKES

2 Screeding the crushed stone. When the first row has been filled, rest a 12-foot section of an extension ladder on the screed strips and pull it down the row to level the stones. Use rakes to pull the ladder and if it seems too light, place pieces of scrap wood over the rungs and weight the ladder down with concrete blocks.

3 **Compacting the crushed stone.** For a porous
court, use a 1,000-pound water-ballast roller
to compact the crushed stone, working down the
row lengthwise and crosswise. For an asphalt
court, which needs a firmer base, hire a paving
contractor to compact the stone with an 8-ton
powered roller. The level of the compacted stone
should be at least ½ inch lower than the tops
of the screed strips; do not roll over the strips.

When the crushed stone is compacted, bring
the base up to the height of the screed strips by
spreading stone dust over the stone. Use shovels and rakes to get the dust roughly level, then
screed it with a ladder as in Step 2.

4 **Removing screed strips.** When the base has
been completed in the first row, fill the 1-foot border left at the inside edge of the curb with layers of crushed stone and stone dust, using shovels
and rakes to smooth each layer. Then remove
the screed strip nearest the curb and reuse it to
form another screed row about 10 feet farther
in toward the middle of the court. Shovel stones
and stone dust into the furrow that is left by the
removal of the strip.

Continuing in the same way, lay crushed stone
and stone dust across the rest of the court,
moving and reusing the screed strips. When filling
the last row at the far side of the court, leave
another 1-foot border next to the curb, to be filled
separately, as before.

When the entire base is laid, check the level of
the court very carefully at all the internal grid
points with a transit level and leveling rod.
Check for unevenness across the court by pulling
a nylon string taut over the surface. Correct
any unevenness greater than ⅛ inch by adding or
removing stone dust. The top layer of a tennis
court—whether it is porous or nonporous—must
be laid over an almost perfectly even base. At-
tempts to compensate for errors by making cor-
rections in the final surface will cause uneven
drainage and uneven settlement.

Choosing a Surface for the Court

Choosing a surface for a tennis court is a complex problem. Dirt and clay are least costly and are easy on the legs and feet, but they need almost daily care and will stain the ball unless they are topped with a 1/10-inch layer of a fast-drying surfacing material, which should be renewed annually. For even better drainage and durability, lay a 1-inch layer of this material directly on the stone base.

Among such surfacing materials are a special crushed red brick, which can be ordered from the Binghamton Brick Company, Binghamton, New York, and a crushed greenstone that is mixed with a binding agent. The latter is made by the Robert Lee Company and by the Har-Tru Corporation, and is sold by suppliers across the country. For a 1-inch layer, you need 40 tons of either material; it will be delivered in about a thousand 80-pound paper bags in two trailer loads. Cover the bags with sheets of plastic to keep them dry until you need them.

Although either one of these fast-drying surfaces can be played on minutes after a heavy rain, they must be swept and smoothed, like dirt and clay, with a broom and roller after every day's play.

An asphalt court not only dries quickly but is almost maintenance-free. Its drawbacks are its unforgiving hardness, the excessive speed it gives to the ball and its cost—you need a skilled asphalt contractor to install the surface in two layers. The initial layer, usually about 2 inches thick, is rough. After it is installed, flood the court surface with water, mark the puddles that are deeper than the thickness of a nickel and have the contractor fill and compact these areas before he spreads the 1-inch leveling layer.

Although you can play on the court after this leveling layer is in place, most people prefer to add at least one coat of asphaltic emulsion to smooth the asphalt, and an acrylic color coat. To make the surface easier on the feet, some people also apply a cushioning coat and, to slow the ball, a gritty texture coat. Both of these are added before the color coat.

For an asphalt court, set the net posts and center net anchor into the court before the finish coats go on. For a porous court, you can set the posts and anchor after the surfacing is complete. The posts for the net must be set at least 2 feet deep *(page 52)* to support the net and prevent frost heave; in harsh climates, set them 3 feet deep. The center net anchor, which holds the middle of the net at the required 36-inch height, is embedded in the center of the court.

When choosing a net, be wary of bargains. The best nets, made of nylon or polyethylene with a vinyl-coated headband, endure bad weather and resist rot better than cotton ones.

Smoothing and Firming a Fast-drying Surface

1 **Screeding the first row.** As a guide to establishing the desired 1¼-inch depth of surfacing material, lay two parallel lengths of steel pipe, 1¼-inch in outside diameter and about 16 feet long, on top of the leveled stone dust; connect lengths of pipe with 1-inch wood dowels. Place one pipe about 10 feet from the brick curb and the other 1 foot from the curb. The 1-foot margin thus created permits you to manipulate the screeding ladder without interfering with the curb. At the end of the court, for the same purpose, lay a 1¼-inch-thick board between the two pipes, 1 foot in from the curb.

Pour nine bags of fast-drying surfacing material into the row every 6 feet and distribute it with a rake until it is slightly more than 1¼ inches deep. Screed it down to this level by pulling a ladder over the pipes. To save on pipe, you can work with shorter lengths, moving the pipes and boards down the court as necessary.

BOARD

10'

1'

2 **Compacting the surface.** When the entire first row is smoothed, wet it with a garden hose fitted with a nozzle that sprays a gentle, flat mist. Wait 20 minutes for the water to percolate all the way through the court, then roll and cross-roll the row with a 1,000-pound roller. Remove both lengths of pipe before proceeding.

SHEET METAL

3 **Screeding adjacent rows.** After the first row has dried, place a length of 16-gauge sheet metal 12 inches wide on top of the finished row, along the inside edge. Lay a pipe 10 feet from the finished row and place boards at the ends as in Step 1. Pour and rake the fast-drying material down the second row, and level it by pulling the ladder over the sheet metal and pipes. Move the sheet metal, pipes and boards as necessary to complete the row, then dampen and roll the surface. Screed the other rows the same way, keeping the fast-drying material 1 foot from the brick curb all the way around the court.

4 **Tapering the court edge.** Pour and rake the fast-drying material into the 1-foot margin around the court. Screed the material with a short length of lumber, using the curb and the hardened edge of the first row as guides, but protect the surface of the hardened edge by placing a piece of sheet metal over it. Because the curb was laid ½ inch below the finished level of the court, the edge of the court will be tapered.

Compact the surface. Rake dirt up around the outside of the brick curb, angling the dirt up to the curb's top outside edge.

A Net Installed to Stay in Place

1 Locating the net and anchor posts. Drive a nail into the court surface at the midpoint of each 120-foot side of the court, just inside the brick curb. Stretch a string between the two nails to indicate the net line. Starting from the outer face of the brick curb—or the edge of the asphalt on a paved court—measure in 30 feet along the net line to locate the position for the center net anchor; drive a nail there as a marker. Measure to the opposite side to verify that the nail is centered. Measure 21 feet from the nail in both directions along the net line to locate the positions of the inside edges of the two net posts; drive nails to mark these positions. Install the posts as shown on page 52.

2 Installing the center net anchor. On a porous court (dirt, clay or a fast-drying surface), remove the marker nail and center the net anchor over the nail hole. Protecting the anchor with a wood block, drive the anchor into the court until its top is flush with the playing surface.

On an asphalt court, dig a hole for the net anchor before the asphalt has completely set, centering the hole over the net-anchor location, and making it 12 inches deep and 12 inches across. Fill the hole with concrete and set the anchor in it. Keep its top about ⅛ inch above the asphalt to allow for the thickness of the finish coats that you will later apply (right).

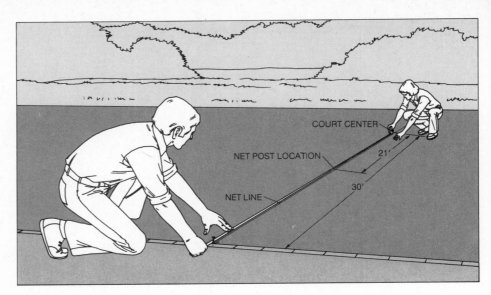

COURT CENTER
NET POST LOCATION
21'
NET LINE
30'

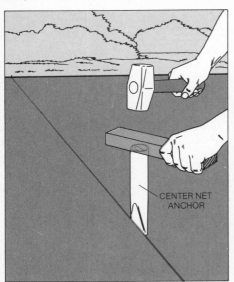

CENTER NET ANCHOR

The Finishing Touches for an Asphalt Surface

Spreading finish coats. Starting at one side of the court, have a helper pour a bucket of the finish—filler, cushion or color coating—down the length of the court as you follow behind, spreading with a 36-inch-wide rubber squeegee. On the first row, angle the squeegee blade about 45° so that any excess flows toward the edge of the court. Overlap all succeeding rows about 50 per cent, and angle the squeegee blade to bring the excess toward the still-unfinished portion of the court. Do not leave ridges of the coating between rows. If the label specifications call for more than one coat, apply each additional coat at right angles to the one beneath it.

Measuring and Laying the Lines of Play

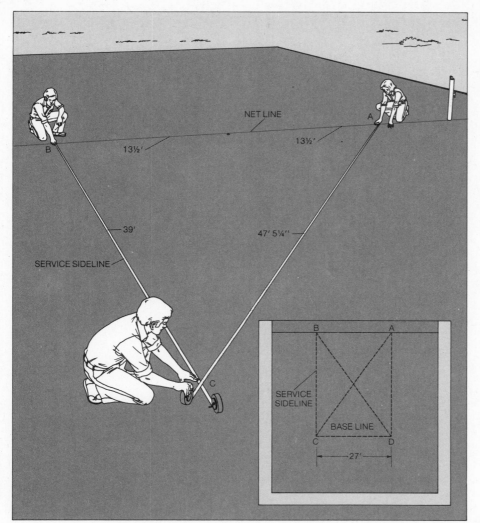

1 Laying out the lines. To determine the sidelines for a singles game, measure along the net line 13½ feet in each direction from its center and drive nails to establish points where the sidelines, also called the service sidelines, intersect the net line—points A and B in the drawing.

To locate one base line, station a helper at point B with a steel tape and extend the tape 39 feet; station a second helper at point A with a second tape extended 47 feet 5¼ inches. Move the free ends of the tapes until they intersect, locating point C on the base line. Locate point D in the same way, reversing the direction of the measurements from points A and B (inset). As a final check, measure the distance between C and D—it should be 27 feet. Drive nails at all four points and stretch string between points A and D, B and C, and C and D.

For the doubles sidelines, extend the net line and the base line 4½ feet in both directions and stretch string between the two points. For the service line, measure 21 feet along the sideline from the net line, drive nails and stretch string between them. Similarly lay out and mark a center line running from the midpoint of the net line to the midpoint of the service line, and a short 6-inch center mark at the midpoint of the base line. Repeat this procedure for the corresponding lines on the other half of the court.

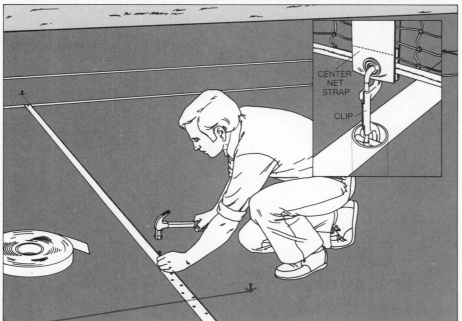

2 Putting down the lines. Fasten a length of line tape to a porous court by stretching the tape along one string, anchoring it at both ends with ten 3-inch aluminum nails driven through the perforations provided for them. (For a court with a cinder or slag base, use copper nails.) Then move to the midpoint of the tape and work back toward each end, setting nails in the holes provided for them. Position center-line tapes over their strings, but place all other tapes just inside the strings, since the strings mark the court's outer boundaries.

Paint lines on an asphalt court by laying two strips of masking tape along the strings, spacing the tapes 2 inches apart; paint between them with acrylic line paint. Position the tapes so that the paint strip falls along the strings in the same way as that described for line tape.

When the court is laid out, attach the net according to manufacturer's instructions and use a spring clip to fasten the grommet at the center of the net strap to the net anchor embedded in the court at the center of the net line (inset).

A Maintenance Routine for a First-Rate Court

The maintenance techniques required to keep a tennis court in tiptop playing condition vary with the court surface. So does the frequency of care. Porous courts of dirt, clay, or fast-drying crushed greenstone and brick dust are constantly wearing away and need regular repair. Asphalt courts are tougher and need only occasional cleaning and patching.

For any new porous court, there is a two-week break-in period, during which the court must be watered every day, brushed with a drag broom and rolled lengthwise and crosswise with a 600-pound water-ballast roller. Thereafter the court needs watering only when the surface looks dry, but should be brushed daily as long as you are playing on it, and after every watering. Also, the line tapes should be swept with a small broom.

In addition to this routine maintenance, a porous court needs special seasonal care. If you live in an area where winters are harsh but there is little snow cover to provide natural insulation—as along the seacoast—the court should be protected from alternate thawing and freezing with a layered blanket of plastic, straw and hardware cloth. When the cover comes off in the spring, the surface should temporarily be roped or fenced off, to keep people from walking on it while it is soft and soggy.

In the spring, too, any porous court will need reconditioning. The depressions should be filled and the entire court top-dressed with the appropriate material. If you have left the court's marking tapes on through the winter—as most people do—you will also need to reset their nails, because frost usually pushes them up. A fast-drying greenstone court should be dressed with about 50 bags of new greenstone. It will also need to be dressed once in the spring and again in midsummer with about 300 pounds of calcium chloride. This restores the bonding agent that holds the greenstone granules together. On the following day the court should be brushed and rolled.

Asphalt courts need very little maintenance beyond an occasional mopping with a mild detergent, and generally last seven to 10 years before they need to be completely resurfaced. If they develop shrinkage cracks, these can be filled with a resurfacing compound sold by the makers of the surfacing material, and leveled with a squeegee. The same compound can be used to fill shallow depressions. When the patches have set, cover them with the same finish coating (page 40) used on the rest of the court.

When asphalt courts develop cracks wider than ¼ inch and depressions deeper than ¼ inch, these generally indicate structural defects in the court's foundation. An entire section may have to be broken up with a jackhammer and rebuilt. Repair jobs on this scale are best left to a contractor, and if the court at the time is more than seven years old, you should probably consider having it completely resurfaced.

Caring for a Porous Surface

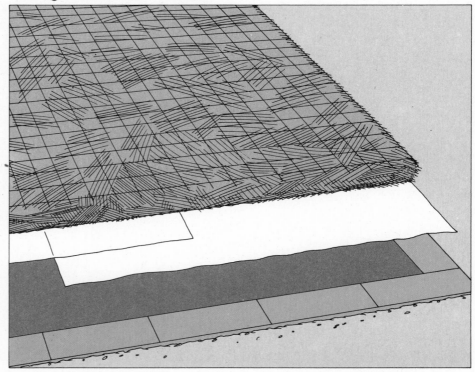

Preparing the court for winter. To prevent frost damage to a porous court that does not get the natural protection of snow, cover the court first with a layer of 4-mil plastic sheets, then with a 2-inch-thick blanket of leaves or straw. Lay the plastic sheets from the low side of the court to the high side (page 34), as you would shingles on a roof, overlapping them about 12 inches. Anchor the layer of leaves or straw with small-mesh hardware cloth to hold it in place.

Patching a depression. Sweep any loose granules out of the depression. With a garden rake, scratch the underlying fast-drying material to a depth of ⅛ inch, and sweep clean. Fill the depression with new fast-drying material and level the surface by pulling a straightedge across it; use a straightedge long enough to span the depression and rest on the undamaged surrounding surface. Water the area and after 20 minutes roll it with a 600-pound roller.

If the depression is more than 3 feet wide, bridge it with a strip of wood whose top surface is flush with the undamaged court surface. If necessary, remove some material from underneath the wood strip so that it sits at the level of the surrounding court. Fill the depression on one side of the wood strip with fast-drying material and level it by drawing a straightedge across it, resting on the side of the depression and on the wood strip *(inset)*. Fill and level the depression on the other side of the wood strip in the same way. Water and roll the two sides and then remove the wood strip and fill the depression left by it.

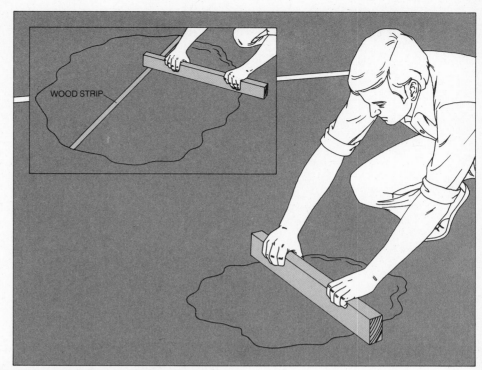

WOOD STRIP

Caring for an Asphalt Surface

Filling cracks. Trowel resurfacing compound into cracks up to ¼ inch deep, smoothing it flush with the surrounding asphalt. Sprinkle sand onto the compound to prevent it from sticking to your shoes while it dries. Wait three days before covering the patched area with the same finishing coats used on the rest of the court.

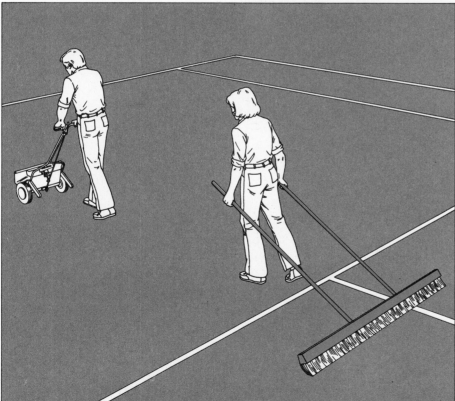

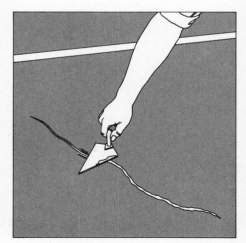

Top-dressing the court in spring. Spread new fast-drying material in lengthwise rows down the newly swept and patched court, using a trough-type fertilizer spreader. Have a helper follow immediately behind the spreader to smooth the material with a drag broom. Spread a second layer in rows across the width of the court. Spray the surface with a garden hose, its nozzle adjusted to a fine mist, until the court is thoroughly damp. Then roll it with a 600-pound roller.

An Ice-Skating Rink from a Garden Hose

Backyard recreation does not have to end seasonally, with the fall foliage. If you live in an area that has freezing temperatures in winter, you can create an ice-skating rink with your garden hose on any suitably large patch of ground. You simply spray water onto the ground in thin layers when the temperature has dropped at least as low as 25°, until you have built up the ice to a thickness suitable for skating. The dimensions of the rink can vary according to the age and seriousness of the skaters, but an area at least 20 by 30 feet is advisable if you hope to accommodate half a dozen ice-hockey players and a homemade hockey goal.

Although a stone-dust court surface is an ideal base for a rink and in other seasons can double as a basketball court, more commonly a home ice rink is built directly over the lawn. The site preparations for the rink vary with the characteristics of your winters. In cold snow country, you can simply clear snow from an area, using the snow to frame the pond, and build up layers of ice on top of the grass beneath. But in regions that are subject to winter thaws, it is better to frame the rink area with a wooden curb and line it with plastic sheeting to prevent the loss of water from melting ice.

Since any rink built over grass, with or without a plastic liner, retards the growth of the grass and may kill it, do not locate the rink in a prominent place on your lawn. You can also take steps in the fall to minimize damage to the grass: Rake up all the leaves, cut the grass very short and refrain from spreading fertilizer over the rink site. If these measures fail and the grass still dies, you will need to re-seed *(page 27)* in the spring.

When choosing a location, consider, too, how to preserve the ice and how to dispose of the water when the ice melts. Try to orient the rink for minimal exposure to the sun, placing it, if possible, so that buildings or trees to the south and west will shade it. Never lay out a skating rink over a septic field, where the ground stays warm, or over soil so sandy that water is absorbed before it can freeze. If you place the rink on high ground, be sure that proper and adequate drainage will be available for the runoff water when the ice melts in the spring.

Constant cold and a gradual build-up of ice are essential for a firm, smooth skating surface. Wait until the ground is frozen to a depth of 2 to 3 inches—usually after three to five days of temperatures lower than 25°—before starting your rink. Then apply the water in thin layers, waiting at least two hours between applications and working only in the early morning or late evening, when temperatures are lowest. Depending on the frequency of applications, it generally takes from three to eight days to build a sheet of good skating ice 2 to 3 inches thick.

Special care in the choice and handling of equipment makes working in cold weather easier. Tire-corded or nylon-corded plastic garden hose—or, if available, rubber hose—remains most flexible at low temperatures. The hose should be drained immediately after each application of water and stored indoors to keep it from freezing; exterior faucets should be turned off indoors, then drained. A heavy coat of paste wax on shovel blades will keep ice and snow from sticking to them.

When the rink is finished and in use, resurface it regularly by pushing away loose ice with a curved scraper and spraying on a thin top coat of water. If you plan to play ice hockey on the rink, you can buy a prefabricated goal or make your own by lacing nylon fishing netting, available at a fishing-supply or marine store, to a frame of rigid plastic pipe, which can be bought at a hardware or plumbing-supply store.

Two Ways to Build a Rink Edging

Banking a rink with snow. Outline the perimeter of the rink by removing a shovel-wide swath of snow, then clear all the snow from the center of the rink, piling it around the edges and packing it tightly with the back of your shovel to form a snowbank. Smooth the surface of the bank by removing any chunks of hard snow or ice, and fill the gaps they leave with loose snow. Sweep the grass lightly with a broom to dispose of any stray lumps of snow.

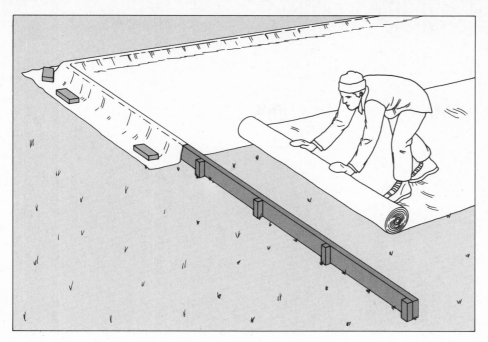

Framing a rink with wood. Before the ground freezes, drive 2-by-2 stakes into the ground to mark the rink perimeter and nail 2-by-6s to them to form a 6-inch-high curbing. Line this frame with sheets of 4-mil or 6-mil sheet plastic. Start at one end of the frame and lay the first sheet down the rink, allowing it to overlap 8 inches beyond the frame on all sides and folding it at the corners for a snug fit. Continue to lay the plastic sheets, allowing a 6-inch overlap between adjacent sheets. Anchor the loose ends outside the frame with bricks or lumber until the first layer of ice locks the plastic in place.

Layering On Water to Freeze by Degrees

1 **Locking the perimeter.** Set the nozzle on a hose for the finest spray and walk around the inside perimeter of the rink, spraying water against the snowbank or the plastic-covered wood frame, giving special attention to corners if a wood frame is used. Take care not to drag the hose over areas that you have just sprayed, and be sure to allow time for the water to freeze solid before continuing.

2 **Layering the surface.** Starting at one end of the rink area, angle the nozzle upward 45° and spray a 2-foot-wide strip all the way across the end of the rink. When you reach the other side, step backward and work in the opposite direction to spray another 2-foot strip, slightly overlapping the first. Work back and forth in this way until the entire surface has been sprayed. Leave this layer for at least 2 hours, until it is frozen solid, before applying the next. Go on spraying at least twice a day until a 2-inch-thick ice base has built up.

To resurface the rink if it becomes rough after use, scrape it with a snow shovel or a curved snow scraper. Then spray a thin film of water over the entire surface.

A Homemade Goal for Ice Hockey

1 **Building a plastic-pipe frame.** For a regulation-sized hockey goal 6 by 4 by 4 feet, use 90° elbow fittings to join 1½-inch rigid plastic pipe into two U-shaped assemblies. Lay the pipe sections, cut square and to length, on the floor to dry-fit them. Mark the joining positions with scratches to allow quick repositioning when you glue. Working in a place where the temperature is above 40°, apply a thick coat of plastic-pipe cement to a pipe end and a thinner coat to the inner surface of its matching elbow; immediately slip the two together, twisting them to spread the glue and align the positioning marks. Hold the joint in place for 30 seconds and wait 3 minutes before gluing the second joint. When both U-shaped assemblies are finished, join them into a frame, using two more 90° elbows (*inset*). Similarly dry-fit, mark and glue the halves.

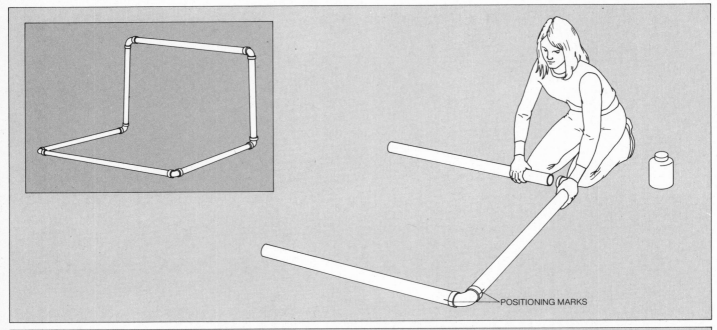

POSITIONING MARKS

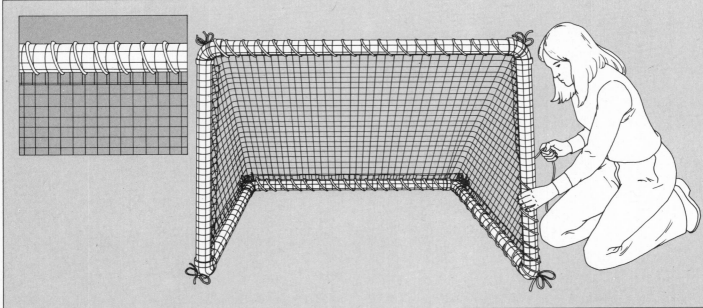

2 **Attaching the net.** Cut a rectangular piece of 1-inch-mesh No. 18 nylon fishing netting measuring about 6½ by 8½ feet, large enough to stretch between and wrap around the 6-foot sections of pipe at the top and bottom of the frame and the two 4-foot angles on the sides of the frame. Anchor the net in position at each corner of the frame with a short piece of nylon cord. Then lace the netting to the frame around all four sides with additional cord, using four separate lengths. Begin by lacing the 6-foot ends, then lace each triangular side. Cut each cord five times longer than the length of the pipe it will wrap, and lace it through alternate squares of mesh on each side of the pipe, skipping every second square (*inset*). When the netting has been secured all the way around the frame, neatly cut away any excess.

One Man's Answer to the High Costs of Tennis Courts

Building a tennis court, like any home-improvement project, involves many decisions about price and quality—or as some might say, about what is essential and what is not. Here, reasonable minds differ. Tennis aficionados—not known for their compromising natures—often observe about homemade courts that "You get what you pay for."

But one aficionado, Bobby Goeltz, a professional tennis instructor in Potomac, Maryland, points with pride to his two fine-looking "poor man's tennis courts" as evidence that you can sometimes get a lot more than you paid for—if you have a good location, put in about 10 days of grueling work, and are willing to cut corners on what some would consider essential. Goeltz built his two courts, one surfaced with native soil, the other with a composite of crushed greenstone and binder, for little more than the cost of 100 hours of playing time at an expensive club. "Everything there is essential," he insists; "everything that is essential is there."

After choosing a site with good drainage and soil that will compact, the first two steps in building any tennis court are to rough-grade it and fine-grade it. "Beyond that, all you need to do is take the rocks out, smooth it and roll it, and the surface is playable," Goeltz says. Sound too simple? In areas with a moist or soft soil, it may be. Yet given a relatively dry soil with a high content of natural clay, grading, clearing and smoothing were indeed all Goeltz had to do to create a playable surface.

The court area was "just a big slope" before the bulldozer cut, filled and rough-graded it. And the bulldozer work, which accounted for one fourth of the cost of the two courts, was the only part of the dirt-court construction Goeltz did not do himself.

At this point, Goeltz made his first—and, he admits, perhaps too hasty—cost-cutting decision. Although he had hired a professional grader to fine-grade the greenstone court, he decided to finish the dirt court himself. First he dragged a steel-edged strip of wood weighted down by cinder blocks across the court with a small tractor; he re-moved rocks from the rough-graded surface by hand. Then he spent several more days working and reworking the surface with rakes, brooms and rollers. Despite this painstaking work, the dirt surface still has visible irregularities that a professional would have eliminated.

The crushed-greenstone court (page 38), a modified version of the quick-drying courts commonly used at tennis clubs, required considerably more work and cost about three times as much as the dirt court. Yet even here Goeltz made some cost- and quality-cutting decisions. Rather than cover the rough-graded surface with the usual drainage layers—4 inches of coarse stone plus ½ inch of stone dust—Goeltz skipped the coarse stone altogether, coating his dirt surface with only the ½ inch of stone dust. On top of this, instead of the recommended 1¼-inch layer of greenstone-and-binder mix, Goeltz settled for a thin, ¼-inch covering.

These rather drastic cuts meant a sacrifice of downward drainage on the greenstone court. But Goeltz contends there were advantages as well. He saved more than 80 per cent on materials. Also, the absence of a crushed-rock drainage layer means that during the area's dry periods the greenstone cover requires less frequent watering. His end-pitched courts drain primarily over the court and into a shallow swale at the lower end rather than, as traditionally, down through the surface of the court. And though his thinner greenstone cover will have to be renewed annually, all porous courts need an annual reconditioning.

Though purists might call these makeshift courts, Bobby Goeltz is quite content with them, as are the partners he plays with three to five hours a day. "The only thing I'd do differently," he says, "is what my father originally told me to do—build two dirt courts and fine-grade them both." That would have halved his expenses, and offered two great advantages in the drainage: If a dirt surface washes off, there is more of the same below, and water drains through the area's soil very well.

To skeptics, Goeltz likes to tell a story. One friend, himself a court contractor, had glibly advised Goeltz that there was no such thing as a cheap playable court. "You just try it," he said. Later, shown the completed courts, the contractor turned to Goeltz, shook his head, and said: "What can I say?" Says Bobby Goeltz, "It was the nicest comment he could have made."

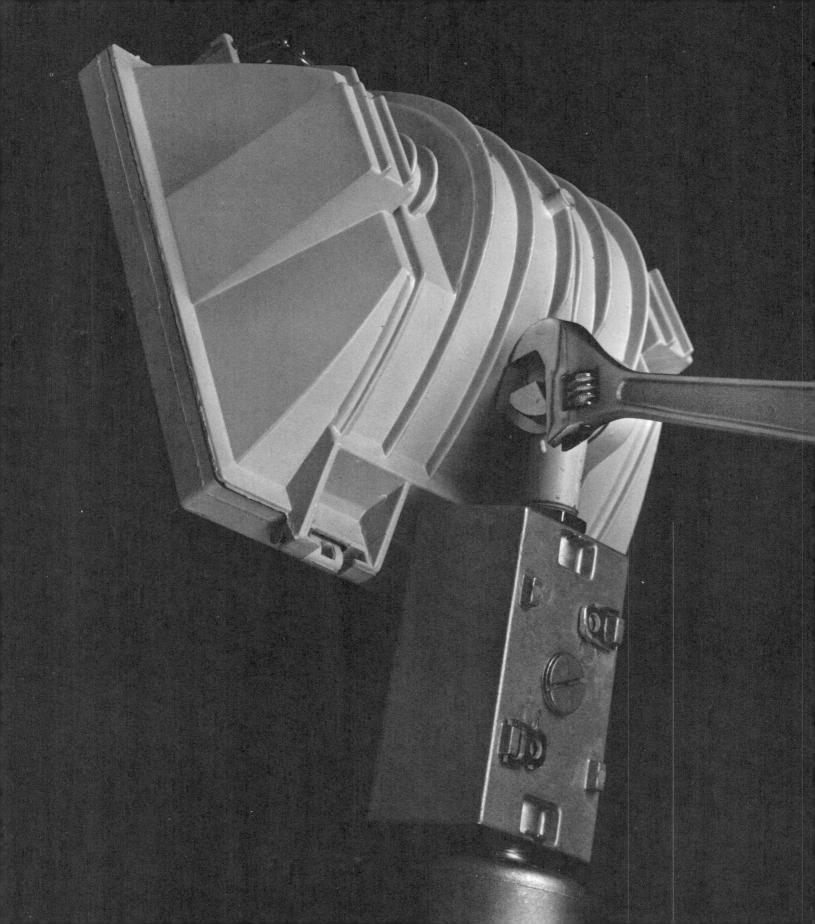

A light for fast-moving games. This swivel-mounted high-intensity quartz floodlight throws even light over a wide area, allowing players to follow the trajectory of a small ball traveling at high speed. Economical to operate because a tube-shaped bulb 4 inches long provides a great amount of light, the fixture is mounted on a weatherproof outlet box atop a metal pole, and can shed its light to a distance equal to twice the height at which it is mounted.

The children of Crete swung on swings in 1600 B.C., the ancient Romans set aside space in public baths for playing catch with air-filled animal bladders, 13th Century French noblemen hung tassled strings in castle courtyards and batted balls over them with the palms of their hands. Equipping places especially for play, for adults as well as for children, has a long and honorable history. True, there have been times when play was scorned as a pastime for lazy idlers—Oxford University students of the 17th Century were fined, imprisoned and even expelled for playing football. But generally man's urge to frolic has prevailed.

Finding a place for outdoor play in today's crowded urban society presents a challenge, but once you have an open piece of ground, the possibilities are many and various, from a solitary tetherball in one corner of a yard to an elaborately equipped, elaborately challenging playground. The work involved in equipping even a complex play area is surprisingly simple—a few techniques go a long way. With the same basic steps, you can set up two posts for a volleyball net or 36 for a backstop fence around a tennis court. With a few bolts and nuts, such posts might also support a rebound net, a basketball backboard, a chin-up bar, a seesaw or a swing.

Beyond the basic building techniques lies the greater pleasure of tailoring a play area to suit your family and your tastes. The nets and courts needed for organized games are to a large extent standardized, but the designing of children's play equipment leaves room for infinite variety. You do not need to settle for a small steel swing set that you fear will topple over with each enthusiastic flurry of activity. With imaginative planning on the part of the whole family, you can create a strong network of playthings for climbing, swinging, sliding, hanging, balancing. Large or small, such a network provides opportunities for children to cooperate, to explore, to develop their imagination, to increase their physical agility—all elements of play that are important in any child's development.

A play area becomes truly complete when it is illuminated for use on a warm summer evening. Here again, a few techniques provide a variety of possibilities. If your goal is to illuminate a tennis court, the steps in choosing and installing bright, glare-free lighting are straightforward. But if optimum visibility is a lesser concern, you can give the play space a nighttime charm all its own with lighting chosen for drama. A lamp hidden in the top branches of a tree will cast a dappled ray of moonlight on a moonless night; the same lamp at the base of the tree would outline a captivating pattern against the black sky. Lights are the final touches that help your play area welcome you whenever you find time to relax.

Posts and Poles: The Basic Support System

Posts and poles are the stiff backbones for many kinds of game and play equipment—nets, backstops, climbing gyms, even windscreens. For these varied uses, two materials prevail: steel and wood. While galvanized-steel posts need little maintenance, wood has the advantage of being better-looking and, if properly treated *(opposite, bottom),* it is almost as maintenance-free as steel. The two materials are equally suited to most situations and either one can be installed temporarily as well as permanently.

Posts vary in their need for strength, depending on their function. In most cases, you can decide for yourself how strong or permanently planted you want your posts to be, but there is one important exception. Posts for tennis-court backstops must be strong enough to support heavy wire mesh and resist high winds. These gateposts, corner posts and end posts, therefore, should be set in concrete; intermediate posts, under less stress, can be set in tamped earth. There are two other rules of thumb: In very cold regions the hole for any post or pole should be deeper than the frost line; and for stability, a post's depth usually should be at least a third of its total length.

Beyond these strictures, it is possible to be flexible. Temporary installations, for example, can often be substituted for permanent ones, and they have one great advantage—when the game or season is over, the posts or poles can be removed and stored out of sight.

Some temporary poles, such as those for badminton or volleyball nets, come already sharpened and are simply hammered into the earth. Such poles—and the metal legs for swings—can be further steadied with ground anchors and cable. A stronger support for temporary posts—and one that always sets them at the correct position and height—consists of buried sleeves into which the posts slide. Metal tennis-net posts—which come as a kit, complete with a pulley-and-crank mechanism—have long used this sleeve system so the posts can be removed for storage in winter. But the same idea is also applicable to wood posts, using a wooden sleeve, and earth rather than concrete to hold it firm.

Plugging the sleeves when they are not in use is simple. A paper cup slipped, right side up, into the hole keeps out leaves and grass for several days; a plastic cup does so indefinitely. For long-term, off-season capping of wood sleeves, you can make a plug of scrap lumber; for steel sleeves you can use threaded pipe for the sleeve and attach a screw-on cap. If you wish to avoid the presence of sleeves in your lawn, even capped ones, you can make mobile poles for light-net games like badminton by fitting a circular piece of plywood into an old tire, filling the center of the tire with concrete and setting in a pole. The finished assembly can be wheeled whenever you please.

Providing a Permanent Footing

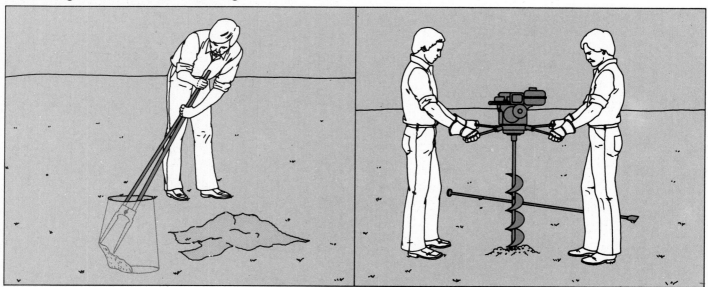

Two ways to dig a hole. For holes as much as 42 inches deep, use a manual posthole digger. Make bell-shaped holes for poles set in concrete, straight-sided holes for poles set in tamped earth. For deeper holes, or when digging many holes, use a two-man gasoline-powered auger, available from tool-rental agencies. Mark the desired depth on the boring bit with masking tape, then apply even pressure as you guide the machine downward. Remove dirt by raising the bit periodically. Clear small rocks away as you encounter them, stopping the motor and digging them up with a shovel or digging bar. If the holes are to be filled with concrete, flare the bottom in a bell shape with a manual posthole digger.

With either digging tool, if you hit a large, immovable rock, do not try to break it; shorten your post and use the rock as a base. Even if it is above the frost line, a large rock is unlikely to be moved by freezing and thawing. However, if this obstruction occurs so close to the surface that your post or pole does not go deeper than 15 per cent of its total length, the post will need two diagonal braces, set to form a right angle—2-by-4s for wood posts, standard cable with auger anchors *(page 53)* for steel posts.

Setting a steel pole in concrete. Fill the post-hole to a depth of 4 to 6 inches with stiff concrete, using a mixture of 2½ parts cement, 3 parts sand, 5 parts gravel, and 1¼ parts (by volume) water. (If you are setting many posts, it may be simpler to order ready-mixed concrete delivered to your house; in this case, have all the holes ready for filling on the same day.) Place a flat rock or a brick on the wet concrete base. Set the pole onto the rock or brick, have a helper check it for height and plumb, then add concrete until the hole is slightly overfilled. Use a trowel to shape the concrete top into a cone-shaped mound so rain water will run away from the pole. Let the concrete set 24 to 48 hours.

Setting a wood post. Fill the bottom of the posthole to a depth of 6 to 8 inches with gravel and top it with a flat rock or a brick. Position the post on this base and check to be sure it is the proper height. For an earth embedment, shovel in the soil, tamping it with a digging bar at 4-inch intervals and adjusting the post to keep it plumb. Fill the hole to overflowing and smooth down the sides of the cone-shaped mound to provide for rain-water runoff. If you decide instead to set the post in concrete, use the method described at left for steel posts.

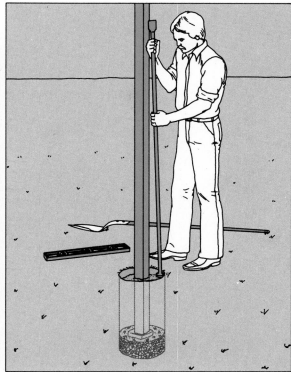

Natural and Man-made Wood Preservatives

Kept dry, lumber does not decay; it is moisture that makes most species desirable food for the fungi whose eating habits cause rot. Wood used outdoors needs strong defenses.

Redwood, cedar and some other woods contain natural toxins that make them unappealing to fungi and insects. However, when posts of these woods are going to be encased in concrete, the portions to be embedded should first soak for two to three hours in a water-repellant preservative because concrete retains dampness.

Other, less expensive woods, like pine and fir, need the protection of chemical solutions. These may be applied under pressure at the factory or, in a less effective but less costly process, brushed on or applied by dipping at home. Pressure-treated wood is far tougher because the solution goes deeper into the lumber; even so, if you drill or saw such lumber, brush the new cuts with a store-bought preservative. Some modern preservatives color the wood green or brown, but most do not release toxic fumes or damage plants. Once it is dry, treated wood can generally be painted or stained.

A Sleeve for Metal Posts

Establishing the sleeve height. Fill the bottom of a posthole with 4 to 6 inches of gravel and measure the depth of the hole from the top of the gravel to ground level, the latter determined by laying a straightedge across the hole. Buy a galvanized-steel pipe approximately this length and ½ inch larger in diameter than the post to serve as the holding sleeve. Tennis-net posts often

come with 2-foot sleeves, but if your soil is loose, dig a 3-foot hole *(inset)* and speed drainage below the sleeve with a slightly larger gravel-filled pipe. Slide the post and its sleeve into the hole until they rest on the gravel, with the top of the sleeve at ground level. Pour concrete around the sleeve, using a carpenter's level to make sure the post is plumb.

Cocking a tennis post. While the concrete is still soft, attach a plumb bob to the pulley at the top of the special post that is designed to hold a tennis net. Tilt the post about 5° out of plumb, away from the court, gauging the angle by the position of the plumb bob; its center should hang 2½ inches clear of the post at ground level. Cocking the post will help counter the tension created by the net when it is tightened.

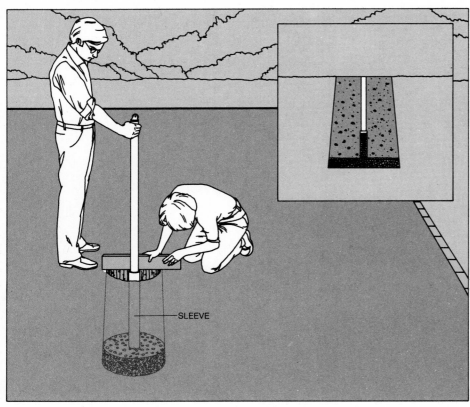

SLEEVE

A Sleeve for Wood Posts

1 Building a sleeve of wood. With galvanized nails, nail four 1-by-8s, pressure-treated to resist rot, to make an open-ended box; allow a ½-inch clearance in the center opening so the post will slide easily in and out. For a 3½-inch-square post, the actual size of a 4-by-4, the sleeve opening should be 4 inches square. Since the 8-inch-wide boards project at each corner of the box, they will serve as stabilizing wings when the box is set in the earth. To fashion a plug *(inset)* to use when the post is not in place, nail a square piece of ¾-inch-thick lumber, 2 inches larger than the outer dimensions of the sleeve, to a 6-inch section of post lumber.

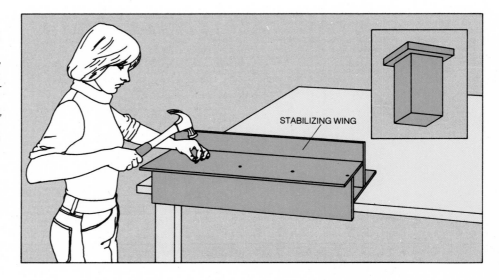

STABILIZING WING

2 **Setting a wood sleeve in the ground.** Fill the bottom of the posthole with 6 inches of gravel. Push the bottom of the wood sleeve against the gravel base and slide the post into it, adjusting post and sleeve for plumb by holding a carpenter's level against two adjacent sides. Fill in around the sleeve with earth, tamping the earth against the stabilizing wings with a shovel.

An Auger to Anchor Unstable Frames

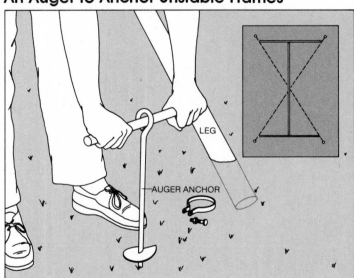

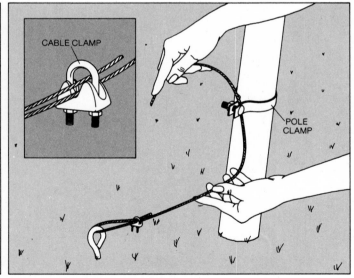

1 **Setting the anchors.** To stabilize the diagonal supporting legs of a metal swing, run a cable from each leg to an auger anchor, which you screw into the ground by turning a metal bar inserted through the anchor eye. Position each anchor 6 to 8 inches outside the leg, lining up the anchor with the leg and with a point directly beneath the midpoint of the swing's horizontal supporting bar *(inset, top view)*. Screw the anchor into the ground clockwise until its eye is about 3 inches above the ground. If, with time and constant use, the anchor becomes loose, tighten it by screwing it farther into the earth or by relocating it slightly out from its original position.

2 **Attaching the cable.** Slide a pole clamp around the post 6 inches above ground level, and insert a bolt through the holes in the arms of the clamp. Run a length of 20-gauge 6-stranded steel cable through the anchor eye and secure it with a cable clamp *(inset)*. Then loop the cable through the opening between the arms of the pole clamp, pull the cable taut and hold it with a second cable clamp. Tighten the bolt on the pole clamp, pulling the clamp arms together to hold the cable firmly. Trim the cable ends and cover them with a binding of cloth adhesive tape. Mark the cable with brightly colored yarn or cloth to remind children of its location.

Outdoor Lights to Lengthen the Period of Play

Few things are more frustrating in outdoor sports than not being able to see the ball or boundary lines when daylight fades. But darkness need not spoil your fun. Installing an outdoor recreational lighting system involves little more than tapping power from a new or existing circuit, running the new cable to an inside wall switch, then taking it outside to new lighting fixtures mounted on or some distance away from the house.

To begin, list the activities you want to illuminate, because lighting requirements vary for different sports. Slow-motion games such as croquet, horseshoes or shuffleboard, as well as children's play areas, can be adequately lighted with 5 footcandles of illumination. This can generally be provided with a low-voltage garden-lighting system operated from a step-down transformer. But fast-action games such as tennis, badminton or basketball require at least 10 footcandles, which is more than a low-voltage system will efficiently provide.

Footcandle computation involves a complicated formula. There is one rule of thumb—an incandescent floodlight mounted 15 feet high requires 6½ watts of power per square foot to achieve 5 footcandles of illumination on the ground. But this is a generalization only; variables such as shadows or street-light glare must be considered. There are only two sure methods of attaining precise illumination. The first is the trial-and-error procedure of installing fixtures, then testing the results with a light meter. The second is to get an expert's advice while your project is still in the planning stage.

Intensity of lighting, however, is only one factor to consider. Another is the quality of the light—its color, amount of glare, level of contrast and evenness of distribution over the playing surface. For example, in most cases mercury-vapor lamps will produce too much glare for tennis, and quartz lamps will be too bright for shuffleboard.

The cost of the various systems—in terms of installation, maintenance, operation and replacement—is a third, and critical, consideration. Mercury-vapor fixtures and lamps, for example, have a high initial cost compared with incandescent floodlights, but this expense must be balanced against the economy of a life span up to 12 times as long and a highly efficient use of electricity.

Once you have chosen the type and number of bulbs you need, determine whether you can safely tap into existing circuits. To do this, add the number of watts required for the new bulbs and divide by 120 volts. The result, in amperes, should not exceed 12—and then only if the circuit still has substantial unused capacity. If you install several high-powered 1,500-watt quartz fixtures, you will need to have a new circuit installed by an electrician, and perhaps a new service panel as well. Also, depending on your local code, this work may require that you obtain a permit.

Zoning regulations and the location of neighbors may also affect the height and type of fixture you use. High-intensity floodlights on 35-foot poles can quickly alienate the best of neighbors if the lights shine into their yards—and lights mounted at such a height may be illegal.

When you are ready to begin work, make certain that power in the circuit you will be working with has been shut off. If you will be running cable underground, have sufficient lengths of UF cable—a plastic-sheathed cable designed to be buried directly in the earth—plus enough conduit to shield exposed cable up to 8 feet above the ground to protect it from accidental abrasion. Where cable runs into metal pipe, smooth the inside edges of the pipe's ends with a file to prevent damage to the cable.

If you plan to install outdoor receptacles, all wiring running to them must be protected by a ground fault interrupter (GFI), which can be part of these receptacles or part of the circuit breaker protecting the circuit. This sensitive circuit breaker, designed to give extra protection to circuits in damp places, is expensive but worth the safety it provides.

In many cases, a circuit can be tapped in an unfinished basement or garage, allowing you to run indoor extensions along studs or joists. In finished rooms, where exposed cables would be unsightly, you can run cable on the surface of a wall through a system of protective channels known as raceway. If on the other hand you decide to put the cable inside a finished wall, a fish tape that you use to pull the cable through (page 59, Step 3) is a great convenience.

If long trenches outside will be required, consider renting a power trencher. At times, a cable may have to pass beneath a walk. If so, dig a trench on one side first, then dig on the other side. Hammer an end of a length of rigid conduit to a sharp, closed point, drive it under the walk with a maul to join the trenches, then cut off the closed end of the conduit with a hacksaw so you can feed the UF cable through it.

A recreational lighting system. Though few houses will have the exact arrangement of this example, its basic lighting plan can be applied to many situations. The two-directional incandescent floodlights over the garage door illuminate a basketball backboard and play area along the driveway. Low-voltage mushroom fixtures light a children's play space that can be supervised from the house. A mercury-vapor fixture mounted on the side of the house efficiently casts a wide area of light for volleyball and badminton. Farther from the house, quartz fixtures on tall posts evenly illuminate a tennis court. (The intense concentrated beams provided by spotlights are rarely used in recreational lighting.)

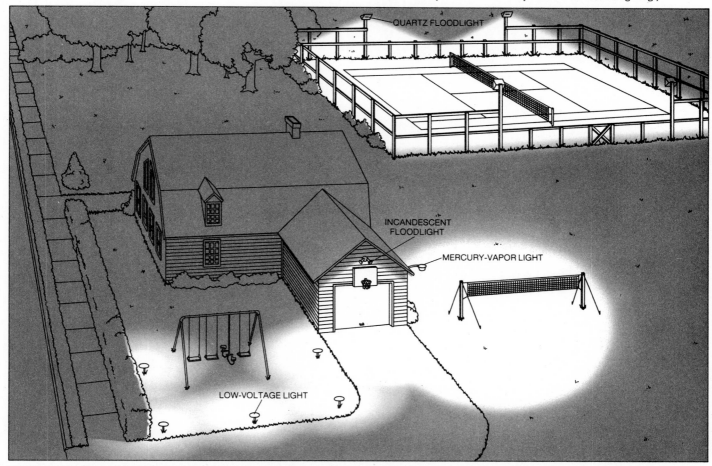

QUARTZ FLOODLIGHT

INCANDESCENT FLOODLIGHT

MERCURY-VAPOR LIGHT

LOW-VOLTAGE LIGHT

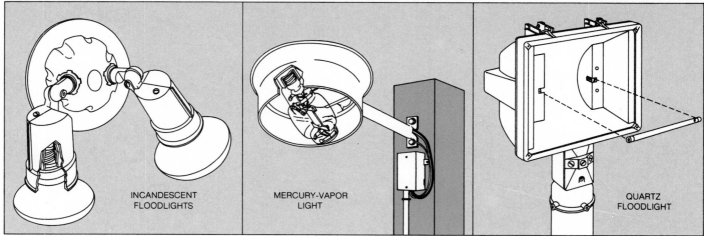

INCANDESCENT FLOODLIGHTS

MERCURY-VAPOR LIGHT

QUARTZ FLOODLIGHT

Three types of recreational lamps. Incandescent fixtures are lowest in initial cost and easily adjustable, to change lighting direction. Their bulbs are easy to replace and provide good color, but they last only about 2,000 hours and are expensive to operate. Mercury-vapor lamps last upward of 24,000 hours and provide a great deal more light per watt than incandescent bulbs, but they give off an unnatural, whitish light that cannot readily be aimed, and they require about 10 minutes to build up to full intensity. Quartz fixtures are expensive initially, but their lamps produce a warm, natural light and are more economical to operate than incandescents; they last approximately 4,000 hours.

Mounting Light Fixtures High on the House

1 **Tapping power.** With the power off, connect the wires of existing cables in a junction or outlet box to the wires of a new cable leading to a new switch location. First remove a circular knockout from the box, install a cable connector with a clamp in the knockout hole and secure the connector with a lock nut. Then push the new cable into the box and tighten the clamp onto it. Match the old and new wires—black with black, white with white, and bare copper ground wire with the bare or green wire. Cover the wire ends with wire caps and replace the cover.

From outside the house, drill a 1-inch hole at the planned location of the new fixture. Run a cable from the indoor switch location to the hole.

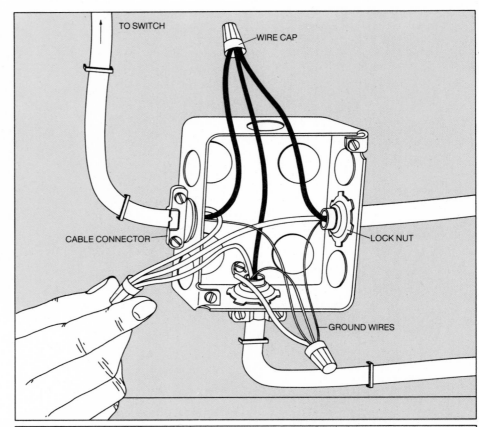

TO SWITCH

WIRE CAP

CABLE CONNECTOR

LOCK NUT

GROUND WIRES

2 **Adding an inside wall switch.** After attaching cables from the junction box and the fixture location to a switch box, set the switch box into a wall opening. Then connect the white wires to each other. Connect the two ground wires from the cables to each other and add two short green-insulated or bare jumper wires to them. Connect one of the jumper wires to the back of the switch box, the black wires to the two screws on the side of the switch (*as shown here*). Connect the second ground jumper to the green screw on the switch. Fasten the switch to the box with mounting screws, then fasten the cover over it.

If you are working with a plaster, wallboard or paneled wall, cut a hole the size of the box between studs, set the box into the hole and, holding it in place with one hand, insert brackets on one side at a time, between the box and the wall opening. Pull each bracket toward you as far as possible, then bend its arms into the box. Squeeze the bend tightly with needle-nose pliers to hold the box snugly in place.

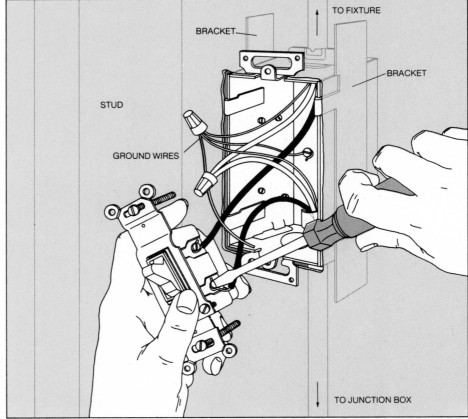

TO FIXTURE

BRACKET

BRACKET

STUD

GROUND WIRES

TO JUNCTION BOX

3 **Connecting to an outdoor box.** Outside the house, slip a cable connector over the cable end and, holding the connector with pliers, screw a weatherproof outlet box onto it, using the threaded hole in the back of the box. Set the connector into the 1-inch hole in the house and use wood screws through the box's mounting tabs to secure the box *(inset)*.

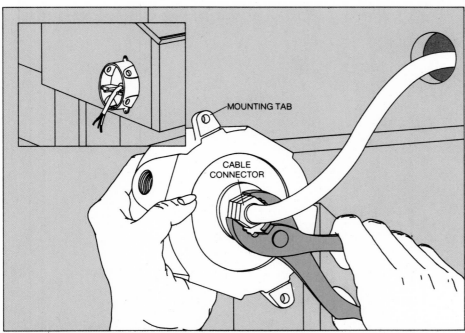

MOUNTING TAB

CABLE
CONNECTOR

4 **Wiring and mounting the fixture.** Connect the two white fixture wires (if you are installing a double fixture) to the cable's white wire, and the black fixture wires to the cable's black wire. Connect the bare ground wire to the ground screw in the outlet box. Align the holes in the fixture, the gasket and the outlet box and fasten with the machine screws provided. Adjust the bulb housings to the desired positions, then tighten the lock nuts. Set gaskets onto the bulb sockets and screw in outdoor-type floodlight bulbs. Turn the power back on.

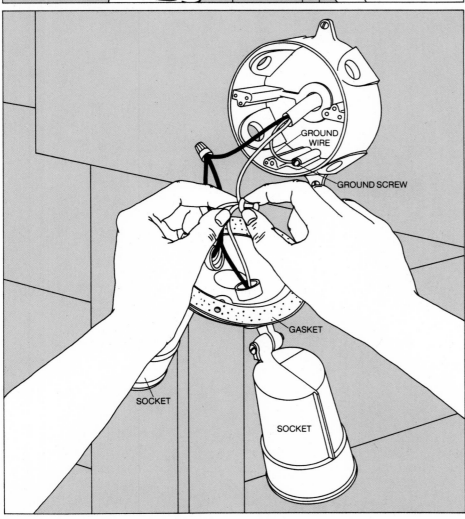

GROUND
WIRE

GROUND SCREW

GASKET

SOCKET

SOCKET

Installing Court Lights on Wood or Metal Posts

1 **An exit through an outside wall.** Dig a trench 12 inches deep, from the place where the wiring will leave the house to the post location. Drill a ⅞-inch hole—at least 3 inches from the sill plate, flooring and any regular joist—through a header joist above the trench. Screw a threaded nipple long enough to pass through the hole and into a junction box, into one end of an LB fitting; into the other end, screw a piece of conduit long enough to reach about 6 inches into the trench. Screw a short length of ½-inch rigid coupling fitted with a cable connector into the open end of the conduit. Push the nipple through the hole in the header joist and strap the conduit to the foundation, using offset circular clamps and screws with lead anchors. Caulk around the nipple.

To drill a cinder-block wall, use a ⅞-inch star drill. Choose a spot in the second course below the siding, over a block's hollow center. Rotate the drill an eighth turn after each hammer tap to make a round hole. Measure carefully and match the outside hole on the inside of the block.

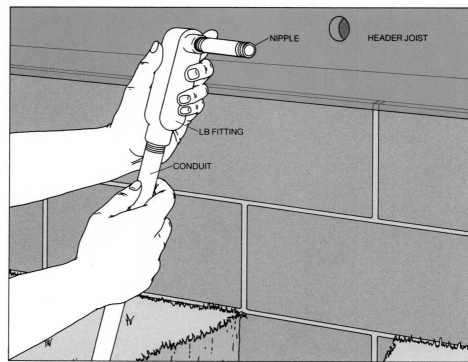

NIPPLE   HEADER JOIST

LB FITTING

CONDUIT

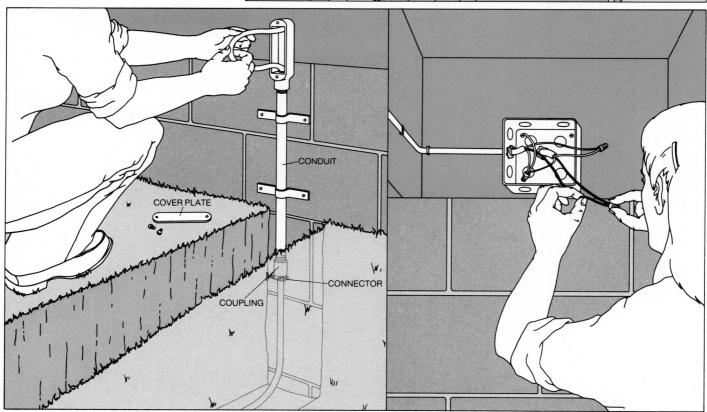

CONDUIT

COVER PLATE

CONNECTOR

COUPLING

2 **Feeding cable to the box inside.** Remove the cover plate and gasket from the LB fitting and feed a UF cable from the trench up through the conduit into the fitting. Then bend the UF cable and push it through the nipple into the house.

Inside, attach a 4-inch-wide junction box to the end of the nipple, tightening a ½-inch lock nut on the threaded nipple inside the box. With the power off, connect white, black and ground wires of the UF cable to the identical wires of a

length of cable connecting the box to the new inside wall switch (*Step 2, page 56*). Connect a jumper ground wire from a screw in the box to the other ground wires. Attach the cover of the box with the screws provided.

3 **Running cable up an outdoor post.** Using a steel post, run a fish tape down from the top and out a predrilled hole near the bottom. Push a short piece of rigid ½-inch pipe into the hole to protect the cable. If the post has no hole, drill a ½-inch hole 12 inches below the point where the post will emerge from the ground. Connect the fish tape to the UF cable (*inset*) and pull the cable out the top of the post. If the post is already set in concrete, drill an entry hole as low as possible. Then run the cable from the trench to the entry hole inside a piece of conduit anchored to the concrete and fish the cable up through the pole as before.

On a wood post, there is any easy alternative to conduit for protecting cable where local codes permit. Use a router to make a groove ½ inch wide and deep up the side of the post, then wedge the cable in the groove from the trench to the fixture location. To secure the cable, hammer staples every 12 inches over the groove.

FISH TAPE

PIPE

CABLE

GROOVE

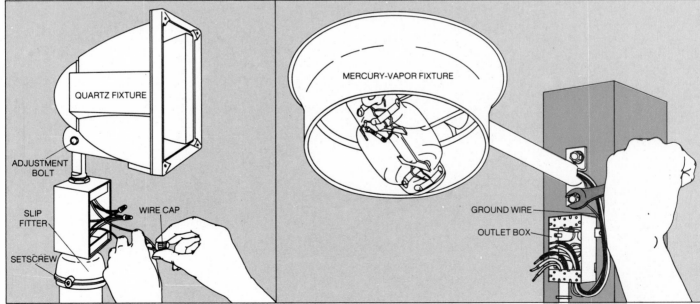

QUARTZ FIXTURE

ADJUSTMENT BOLT

SLIP FITTER

WIRE CAP

SETSCREW

MERCURY-VAPOR FIXTURE

GROUND WIRE

OUTLET BOX

4 **Wiring and attaching a fixture.** For a steel post and a quartz-fixture connection, thread the UF cable through a slip-on cap that can be fastened to the post top with setscrews. Thread an outlet box onto the slip-on cap and attach the light fixture to the outlet box by screwing the threaded nipple extending from the fixture bottom into the top of the outlet box. Then make the wire connections. Screw the cover onto the outlet box and tighten the bolts on the back of the fixture to aim it.

With a wooden post and a mercury-vapor fixture, bolt the fixture to the post with lag bolts and mount a threaded weatherproof junction box with two cable connectors on the bottom onto the post below the fixture. Run a bare grounding wire, along with the black and the white fixture wires, into the outlet box, taping the three wires together where they enter the connector. Then connect the ground wire to the fixture lag bolt. Inside the box, connect the fixture and ground wires to the corresponding cable wires with wire caps. Cover the box and restore power.

The Dividers and Barricades: Nets and Fences

Providing a fence around a recreation area may be a matter of safety, convenience, comfort, esthetics or some combination of these considerations. For example, because a swimming pool is considered an "attractive nuisance," dangerous to small children, many communities require that any pool be surrounded by a security fence. Such security fences usually must meet certain specifications—typically, that they be at least 4 feet high, not climbable, and equipped with a lock that no six-year-old can open.

However, many fences perform less critical functions, such as providing privacy, blocking the wind or sun, keeping balls within easy retrieval range, or simply beautifying the recreation area.

Public courts and playing fields usually are enclosed by chain link fencing. By far the most durable wire fence, it is also the most expensive, and because of its weight it is difficult to install at heights of more than 6 feet. For home use, fences and backstops made of wood or of wire stretched over a wood framework are often the best choices. They are relatively inexpensive, are easy to install, and can be quite attractive, particularly if they are covered with climbing vines.

The most time-consuming part of building a wood fence is sinking and anchoring the posts *(pages 50-51)*. But once these are set, the job can be completed quickly. In just a couple of days, a team of two can complete the wood framework and attach wire fencing for a standard tennis-court backstop 60 feet wide and 120 feet long. The posts themselves should be 6 or 8 inches in diameter or 4 or 6 inches square, and should be sunk every 6 to 10 feet at a safe distance beyond the playing surface *(page 132)*. Be sure the lumber is dry, seasoned and pressure-treated; otherwise the posts may warp after they are sunk and pull the framework out of line. To complete the skeleton, connect the posts with horizontal rails of 2-by-4s or 1-by-6s.

Wood panels, boards, or lightweight wire fencing—16- to 20-gauge—can be attached to such a framework to create anything from a solid privacy fence to a mesh backstop through which spectators can watch the game. Chicken wire, the least expensive wire fencing, is also the most likely to bow and sag at the bottom. Weaving galvanized tension wires through the base of the fence and tying them to the foot of the posts will help to hold it tight. A chicken-wire fence can be expected to last seven or eight years, but even if it had to be replaced annually for 20 years, it would still be less costly than chain link fencing. This makes chicken wire worth considering, particularly if the fence will not be subjected to hard use.

More durable than chicken wire is hardware cloth—a screen-like wire fabric with a square mesh ¼ to ½ inch wide. It is more unwieldy, however, and costs about four times as much. Another alternative, which costs half again as much as chicken wire, is 16-gauge galvanized fencing wire with a 2-inch-by-3-inch rectangular mesh. Tough and flexible, it is available in either plain or vinyl-coated finishes at most hardware stores.

Vinyl-coated wire fencing resists rust much longer than plain galvanized wire and, if green or black, is also less conspicuous. But you can achieve much the same results by coating the plain version with oil-based exterior paint.

After your fence or backstop is installed, you may want to hang windscreens on it. Usually made of polypropylene or of vinyl-coated polyester, a windscreen not only breaks the force of the wind but increases privacy, reduces visual distractions and provides a dark background that makes it easier to see a ball in flight. The degree to which it performs these functions depends on the tightness of the mesh. For mounting on a wire fence, choose an open-mesh screen or a closed-mesh screen broken at intervals by air vents. A strong wind beating against a completely closed-mesh screen can bring down even a chain link fence.

For the same reason, the top and side edges of windscreens should be attached to the fence with break-away devices. The least expensive fasteners are self-releasing plastic ties that will break under stress, detaching the windscreen from the fence before any damage is done. The screen's bottom edge should be attached with galvanized-steel S hooks to keep the screen from blowing away.

In ordering windscreens, measure your finished fence or backstop and divide it into sections, always stopping at corners. For convenience in handling, make no screen more than 60 feet long. Windscreens typically come in 6- and 9-foot widths but can be ordered in any width, up to the full fence height. Wind conditions and visual distractions in your area will determine what coverage you need.

In areas where wind protection is not necessary, a screen of vines in lieu of a structural windscreen can provide both privacy and a handsome background. A sturdy wood-and-wire fence can easily support Japanese hop vine, English ivy, clematis, silver fleece or trumpet vines. All grow quickly and are easily trained to climb along the wire, although you may have to attach them to the fence with plastic ties to get them started. One disadvantage to a vine-covered fence is that the vines may obstruct replacement or repair of the fencing, should that be necessary. However, several vines—notably silver fleece, clematis, and English ivy—can survive even drastic pruning.

In addition to being surrounded by fences, many court games are divided by nets, the more fragile counterparts of fences. There are also rebound nets, a boon to single players who want to practice their strokes silently, without the constant pock-pock sound of a wooden backboard. Because nets must stand up to the pressure of balls traveling at high speed, they are installed in much the same way as fences: strung between posts sunk solidly into the ground at the edges of the playing surface.

A Backstop of Wood and Wire

Enclosing a tennis court. Backstops for a tennis court can surround the court, or can simply bracket its ends, backing up the end lines and extending 20 or 30 feet along the sidelines. Backstops for the end lines and for the first 20 feet of each sideline should be 10 to 12 feet high. Sideline backstops can step down to as low as 4 feet in the center.

The backstop shown is supported by a framework of 4-by-4 wooden posts set 10 feet apart and as far from the playing surface as possible, up to

the regulation 21 feet of back space at each end and 12 feet at each side. Posts for the high sections of the backstop are 15 feet long and are buried 3 feet deep in the ground, giving them an above-ground height of 12 feet. The shorter posts are 6 feet long and are set 2 feet deep, giving them an above-ground height of 4 feet. The four corner posts and the two gateposts are set in bell-shaped concrete footings 12 inches wide, to ensure stability; the rest of the posts have tamped-earth footings 10 inches in diameter. The horizontal rails are lengths of 1-by-6.

A simple frame of 2-by-4s with a diagonal brace forms a side gate. Galvanized-steel fencing wire with 2-inch-by-3-inch mesh is attached to the framework with 1-inch fence staples.

An alternate design (*inset*) uses "California corners"—10-foot-long sections set at an angle of 135° to the end line and sideline—instead of the usual right-angle corners. Here, the end-line backstop is 40 feet long, the sideline sections 10 feet long. The California corner saves materials and keeps stray balls closer to the players.

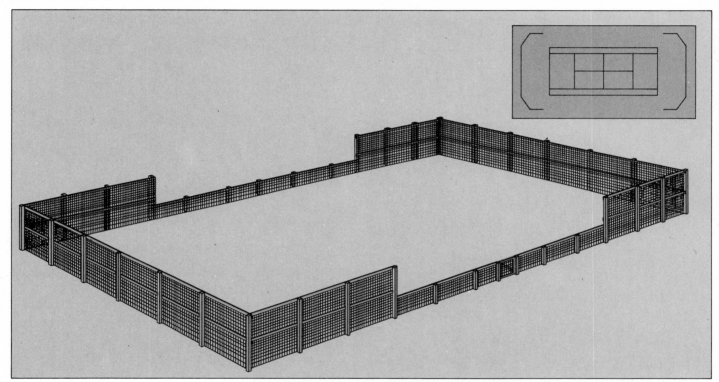

1 Building a framework. Working on the court side of the fence posts, position the upper rail so it is level and as nearly flush as possible with the tops of the posts. While a helper holds it level, attach the rail to the posts with galvanized nails at each end. At corners, screw the second rail to the first, using three 3-inch corner brackets, two on the side facing the court and one centered on the other side (*inset*).

Cut the rails to meet at the midpoint of the posts, except at the corners, where one rail should extend across the post and the second rail will butt against the face of the first (*inset*). When the upper rails are in place, mark for the lower rails by measuring down 69 inches from the top edge of the upper rails. Draw a line there and level the top edge of the lower rails against it, attaching them as you did the upper rails.

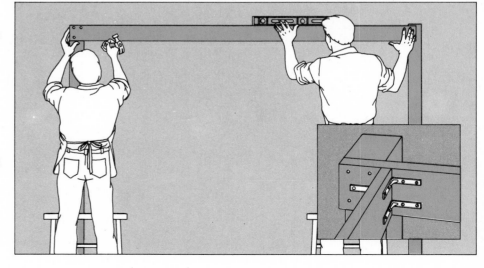

2 **Tacking wire to the upper rail.** Working with a helper, unroll the fencing and tack it roughly in place along the upper rail, lining up the edge of the fencing with the top edge of the rail. Have your helper support the weight of the wire as you work, and place the staples at 2- to 3-foot intervals. Wear gloves to protect your hands while handling the fencing.

At corner and end posts, cut the fencing at a vertical wire, leaving an even edge that extends about 6 inches beyond the edge of the post. This surplus allows you to make adjustments later when you stretch and straighten the fencing; ultimately it will be wrapped and stapled around the posts. Use wire clippers to cut the fencing.

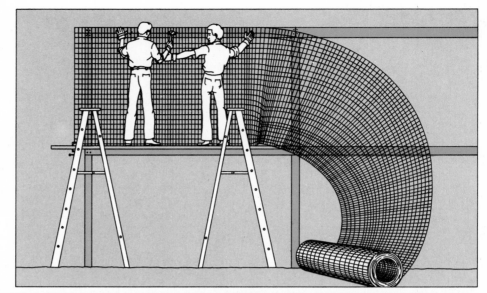

3 **Stretching and stapling fencing.** Fasten the wire fencing permanently to the wood framework by stapling it every 4 inches, first down the center of the posts, then along the top and bottom edges of the rails. Staple the wire to the top half of the backstop first, then to the bottom half. As you work, have a helper stretch the wire taut and align its rectangular mesh with the lines of the framework. If necessary, pry out some staples to make final adjustments. On the posts, place the staples diagonally over the mesh intersections; on rails, set the staples horizontally.

On the lower half of the backstop, staple the wire first to the end post, overlapping the post by 6 inches, then along the top and bottom edges of the rail. Leave a ¼-inch clearance at ground level, if necessary overlapping the upper and lower sections of fencing where they meet.

4 **Wrapping a corner post.** When you reach a corner post in the final stapling, trim away the top 5½ inches of the wire so it butts against the rail of the adjoining fence section. Cut the rest of the wire so there is enough to wrap around the far side of the post. While a helper holds the fencing taut, staple it in place down the front, then down the far side of the post.

5 **Joining lengths of fencing.** To connect two lengths of fencing at a corner post, first wrap and staple the edge of one length to the post. Then notch the other length so that the top of it butts against the adjoining rail and the remainder loosely overlaps the attached fencing by one rectangle. Snip an inch from each section of the last unattached vertical wire. Then lift the snipped sections up and through the openings in the fixed fencing. While a helper stretches the fencing and holds it taut, staple the snipped wire ends to the side of the post.

If a roll of fencing happens to end between corners, make a splice at an intermediate post *(inset)*. A few feet before you reach the post, stop stapling the old roll to the rail, and wrap and staple the edge of a new roll of fencing around the post. Then cut the old roll so one rectangle of mesh will wrap around the far side of the post. Snip out sections of the last vertical wire, as at the corner, and finish the same way.

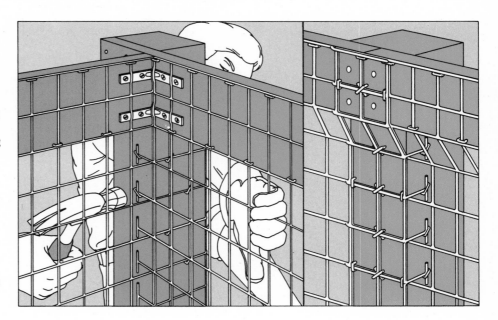

A Gate for a Court Fence

Building a gate. Fasten a rectangle of fencing to the gate frame with staples every 3 or 4 inches along the edges and brace of the frame. Cut the wire so its edges are at least ¼ inch inside the frame edges. To build a rectangular frame with a diagonal brace *(inset)*, use 2-by-4s set on edge and follow the techniques illustrated on page 67. Allow 2 inches of clearance at the bottom and ½ inch on each side. For a gate 4 to 6 feet high, use one diagonal brace; for a taller gate, add a middle rail and use two diagonal braces.

Hang the gate with the wire facing the court and the top of the brace on the latch side. Attach the hinges and latch on the outside *(page 67)*.

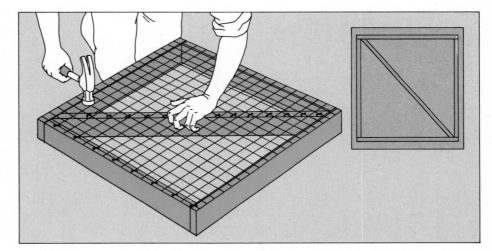

A Screen to Block the Wind

Hanging a windscreen. Starting next to an end post, loop a self-releasing plastic tie through the grommet in one top corner of a windscreen and attach it to a horizontal wire of the fence. Attach the rest of the screen along its top edge with ties looped over the same horizontal wire; then secure the side edges with ties. Adjust the ties so the screen lies flat against the fence, but is loose enough to belly in the wind. Fasten the bottom edge of the screen to the fence with galvanized S hooks, connecting each grommet to a horizontal wire of the fence. Use pliers to close the grommet end of each hook. In a high wind, the plastic ties will break and release the top and sides of the screen, taking the pressure off the fence, while the S hooks will keep the screen from blowing away.

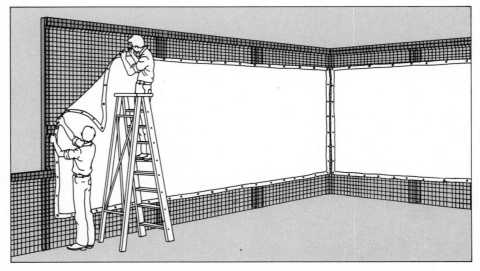

Building a Rebound Net for Practicing

For a tennis player struggling to overcome a weak backhand, or for a softball player eager to improve his pitching, an elastic net that rebounds balls is a welcome extra for a playing area. If such a rebound net is assembled at the court, the problem of transporting it is eliminated. The frame of the net shown is made of 1-inch galvanized-steel pipes from a plumbing-supply store and is designed to span the standard 10 feet between tennis-court backstop posts (*page 61*).

The side rails are 9 feet long; two 1-foot extensions serve as legs. The top rail is 10 feet long and the bottom rail is made of two pipes, 4 feet 11½ inches long, joined in the center. Order the pipes cut to size and threaded at both ends. Join the top corners with two 90° fittings, the bottom corners with two T-shaped fittings and the halves of the bottom rail with a pipe union. Add flanges to the bottoms of the legs.

The net itself, 7 by 8 feet, is made of ¾-inch knotless, weather-treated nylon that will stretch to fit the 9-by-10-foot frame. It has a vinyl binding sewn around the edges and grommets placed at the four corners and every 9 inches around the sides. You can order such a net from a tennis-supply store. The net is laced to the frame with 40 feet of ¼-inch bungee cord, a special elasticized cord that is part of the shock-absorbing equipment in small-aircraft landing gear. It can be bought from aircraft-equipment suppliers; check the classified pages of the telephone directory.

This entire assembly is placed about 10 inches inside the backstop fence. The net tilts slightly; its top rail is about 3 inches closer to the fence than the bottom rail so the ball rebounds at an angle that simulates actual play. Should the net slacken with use, tighten it by pulling up the cords and retying the knots.

Installing game nets is more exacting, since they must be taut enough to keep the top edge virtually level. They can be strung between wood or steel posts set in concrete footings (*pages 50-51*).

Stringing and Erecting the Rebound Net

1 Lacing the net to the frame. Tie the corners of the net to the frame with twine, cut the 40-foot bungee cord in half, then tie the end of one 20-foot piece to one corner of the frame. Working along a 10-foot side, bypass the initial corner grommet and loop the cord through each successive grommet and around the pipe in a continuous spiral. Have a helper do the same with the other 20-foot length of cord, working at the same pace along the opposite side. When you reach the far corner, loop the cord through the corner grommet, around the frame and back through the grommet; then tie a square knot in the cord (*inset*).

Again keeping pace with a helper, work back along the frame to the starting point, pulling the cord tight at each grommet to remove all slack. When you reach the starting corner, untie the cord and loop it through the corner grommet, around the frame and back through the grommet, tying it as before. Cut the cords and use the remaining pieces to lace the other two sides of the net to the frame.

2 Making braces and props. Fasten two predrilled braces to the outside face of each supporting fence post, using ½-inch machine bolts 5½ inches long. Position the pairs of braces 9½ feet and 5 feet above the ground. To make the braces, cut four 2-by-4s 1 foot long and drill a centered ½-inch machine-bolt hole 1¾ inches from one end. In each top brace, drill two ½-inch U-bolt holes in line with the first hole—one 5½ inches and the other 7 inches from the same end.

Set two 1-foot-long 2-by-4 props flat on the ground and toenail them to the fence posts (*inset*). Drive a 10-penny nail 1 inch into each prop, 2½ inches from the outer end.

3 Putting up the net. Set the flanges of the frame's legs over the nails in the bottom props. While a helper steadies the net, U-bolt the top of the frame to the top braces, fastening the nuts loosely. Where the frame crosses the lower braces, outline the sides of the pipe on the wood. Take the net down and drill a pair of ½-inch holes just outside each line. Reposition the net, U-bolt the frame as snugly as possible to all four of the braces, and screw the flanges to the props.

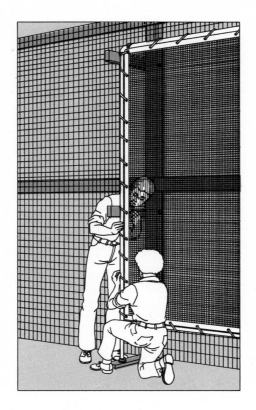

Three Ways to Attach Nets to Support Poles

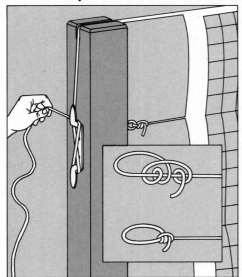

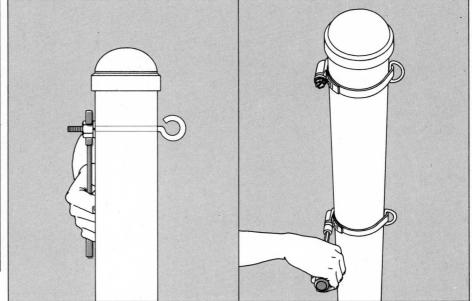

A fastener for wood posts. Using a knife or saw, cut a groove in the top of each post in the direction the net will be strung. On the side of the post facing the court, measure down the width of the net and insert an eye screw. Tie the bottom cord of the net to the eye screw with a tent-hitch knot (inset). If the net has a middle cord, add an eye screw at that height. Screw a cleat to the opposite side of the post. Run the top cord of the net across the groove and down the post, then bind it to the cleat.

Fittings for steel posts. For setting a net at a permanent height, install two eyebolts in each steel post (above, left). For a 3-inch post, use 4-inch-long bolts ¼ inch in diameter. Mark the location of these fittings with a punch and hammer, then drill 5/16-inch holes through both sides of the post. When all holes are drilled, insert bolts and fasten them with self-locking nuts. Set the post in a sleeve or concrete footing (pages 50-52)

with the eyes of the bolts facing the court. For an adjustable fitting that will let you change the height of the net (above, right), slide a metal D ring onto a 3-inch automobile-hose clamp and slip the clamp around the post at the desired height. Tighten the screw on the clamp until the D ring is held securely against the post, facing the court. Such clamps can be loosened and reset to hold the net at any height.

A Privacy Fence that Permits the Passage of Air

A fence design called board-and-board has a three-fold advantage: It is esthetically pleasing, it gives privacy within a recreation area and it permits the flow of air. Moreover, it is very simple to construct. The fence consists of 4-by-4 posts and horizontal 2-by-4 rails sandwiched between vertical 1-by-6 boards. A gate made of the same materials offers easy passage. Use a naturally rot-resistant wood like redwood or cedar or use wood that has been pressure-treated to resist rot; hardware should be galvanized or cadmium-coated.

Before you start building, check your zoning and building codes. Local ordinances may regulate the fence height or its setback from the street, or they may stipulate that a fence that is located on a property line becomes the joint property of both you and your neighbor.

The key to building a strong fence lies in making posts plumb and in setting them in firmly (pages 50-53). Sink each 4-by-4 to a depth at least one third of its total length. Anchor gateposts and corner posts in concrete but if the soil is stable, the remaining posts can be set in well-tamped soil or gravel. Place posts no more than 8 feet apart, positioning them so that a series of 1-by-6s separated by the width of a homemade spacer (Step 1) exactly fills the distance between posts. The placement of gateposts is determined by the width of the gate—between 3½ and 4 feet—plus clearance for the latch and hinges, usually ½ inch and ⅛ inch respectively.

Once the posts are set, use a line level on a taut string (page 15) to level the tops of the posts. Saw off any that are too tall—the post tops become reference points for installing fence brackets to hold the rails. Hang the gate so its bottom clears the ground throughout the arc of the gate's swing.

1 Hanging the rails. Slide 2-by-4 rails into metal fence-rail brackets mounted on the fence posts, placing the upper brackets 9½ inches down from the tops of the posts (inset); make sure each bracket is level by using a try square to draw a line across the post and aligning the bottom of the bracket against it. To position lower brackets, measure down from the top of one post to about 6 inches from the ground; use this measurement to draw lines for the lower brackets on all other posts. Nail the rails to the brackets.

To make a spacer for positioning fence boards, cut a 1-by-4 to fence-board length. Scribe a line 6 inches from one end of the spacer and nail a block of wood to the spacer, with the bottom of the block at the line.

2 Spacing the boards. Hold a 1-by-6 fence board against the rails, with one edge of the board touching a post and the top of the board aligned with the post top; nail the board to the rails. Hook the spacer over the upper rail, using the block as a hanger, and slide the spacer against the first board. Hold a second board against the other side of the spacer, align it and nail it in place. Continue in this way to at-tach boards to the rails, using the spacer and occasionally checking a board for plumb by holding a level against it.

When one side of the fence is completed, similarly space and fasten boards to the other side of the fence. On this side, however, center the first board between the first two boards on the side you have completed.

3 **Making the gate.** Construct a frame for the gate from two 2-by-4 rails cut to fit loosely between the gateposts, two 1-by-6 fence boards and a diagonal 2-by-4 brace. Assemble these elements so the gate rails line up with the rails on the completed fence, using a square to make sure the corners form right angles. Cut the diagonal brace to fit between the two rails, running from the latch side at the top of the gate to the hinge side at the bottom. Fasten the brace to the frame with 4-inch wood screws, two at each end, driving the screws through the brace into the edges of the rails.

Nail fence boards onto the outside of the gate, leaving ⅛ inch between the boards. Then screw the strap sections of two T hinges onto the top and bottom stringers.

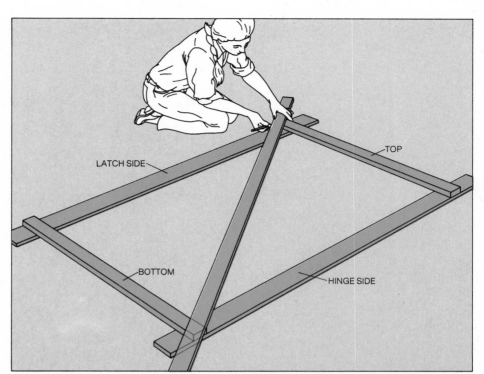

LATCH SIDE

TOP

BOTTOM

HINGE SIDE

STRIKE PLATE

BAR

CHAIN

4 **Hanging the gate.** Mark the positions of the screws for hinges by propping the gate between its posts, using scrap lumber to hold it in position. Align the top of the gate with the top of the fence and set the gate frame flush with the backs of the posts. Drill holes in the post for the hinges and screw the hinges in place.

To attach the latch illustrated (*inset*), first screw the bar onto the gate frame. Then position the strike plate on the post, mark and drill the holes for the screws and fasten the strike plate to the post. To permit operation of the latch from outside the gate, drill a hole through the gate and run a pull chain through it.

A Playhouse of Modular Panels

No child can resist a playhouse, especially one that can be a fort under siege, an enchanted castle, or a spacecraft rocketing its way to Mars. From the child's viewpoint, the less conventional the house the better; from the parents', unconventionality is no problem so long as the house is safe and accessible.

In planning any playhouse, consider the size of its young inhabitants. Two children 8 to 10 years old can play comfortably in a structure that is 4 feet square and has doors and windows scaled to their youthful dimensions. The average 6-year-old is approximately 46 inches tall, a 12-year-old 58 inches. Playhouse doors made to suit this age range are commonly 40 to 48 inches high and windows are 20 to 25 inches from the floor.

For stability, the playhouse should be located on level ground, but before deciding where to put it check the drainage: If rain gathers in puddles near the playhouse door, children will track mud inside. A floor made of loose brick and sand inside and just outside the door will solve this problem. A western or southern exposure gives the best light in the afternoon, when school-age youngsters are most likely to use the house. Local building codes or zoning ordinances may affect the placement and design, with restrictions on height and distance from property lines as well as specific construction requirements.

When you design and construct a playhouse, safety should be a primary concern. Window and door openings are often left uncovered, to provide ventilation as well as light. If a door is added, it is usually hinged so that it swings out. If windows are glazed, they are best covered with unbreakable acrylic rather than glass. In finishing the house, be sure to round and smooth all sharp corners and rough edges with a wood rasp and sandpaper, and countersink any boltheads and nuts that might otherwise project enough to injure children.

The best foundation for a playhouse is one that is both sturdy and removable; you are not likely to want the structure to be permanent. In the playhouse illustrated here, the frame is bolted to stakes made of pressure-treated, rot-resistant wood; these stakes have been set 1½ feet

into the ground. Further stability is provided by plywood panels that project on two opposite sides.

The usual materials for the construction of playhouses are exterior-grade plywood, pressure-treated framing lumber and galvanized bolts and nails. The plywood for the walls can be ⅜ inch thick, but any floor that will have to support youngsters off the ground should be made of ¾-inch plywood. Any of several grades of plywood can be used, depending on the desired appearance, but B-B quality or better will minimize the hazard of splinters.

Power tools, such as an electric drill for making boltholes and a portable circular saw or saber saw for cutting doors and windows, will help speed the work of construction. Weatherproof the finished house with a tinted exterior wood preservative, or with exterior paint applied over a coat of primer. Protect the roof by stapling 6-mil polyethylene plastic over it.

Anatomy of a playhouse. In the two-level house shown here, the walls consist of four plywood panels 4 feet by 8 feet, reinforced with 2-by-4s and bolted to 2-by-2 stakes that have been driven 1½ feet into the ground. Two vertical panels are positioned opposite each other, 4 feet apart and flush against the back horizontal panel. As shown in the bird's-eye view (inset), the front horizontal panel, offset from the back one, is spaced 1 foot away from the vertical panels. This creates 1-foot openings that function as vertical windows at two corners. A fifth reinforced 4-by-8-foot panel rests across the top of the horizontal wall panels, extending 1½ feet beyond each, and serves both as a ceiling over the 4-by-5-foot lower room and as the floor for the upper-level deck.

A rectangular door 24 inches by 43¾ inches, centered in one vertical panel, provides access to the lower room. An interior ladder leads to the upper deck through a 2-foot-square hatch along the 8-foot side of the floor panel, 2½ feet in from its back corner. A safety railing surrounds the upper deck and a slanting roof bridges the vertical panels, providing a sheltered area.

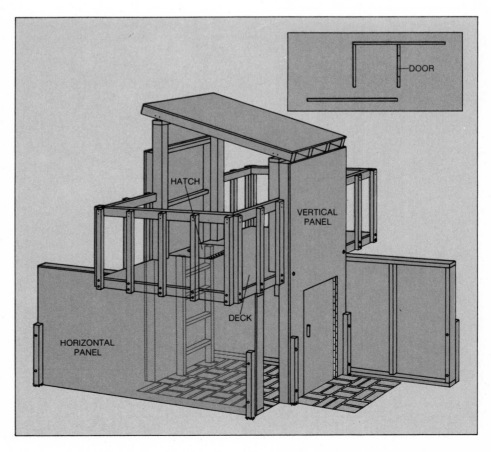

Preparing Sheets of Plywood

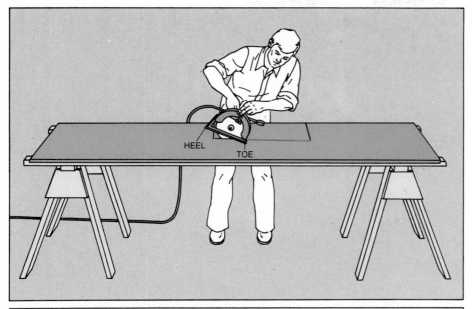

1 **Cutting openings in the panels.** After outlining the door and hatch openings on their panels and cutting along the lines that extend in from the plywood edges, use a portable circular saw— set ¼ inch deeper than the plywood thickness— to make a plunge cut; then saw along the line parallel to the plywood edge. You can also use a saber saw with a plywood-cutting blade. To start the cut with either, turn the saw motor off and rest the base-plate toe on the plywood; hold the saw blade and base-plate heel above the plywood, and position the blade over the marked line. With a circular saw, retract the blade guard, holding it carefully at the top. Start the saw and slowly lower the blade into the wood until the base plate rests flat.

Caution: Hold the saw firmly; turn it off if it jumps. After cutting along all marked lines, finish corners with a keyhole saw and sand all edges.

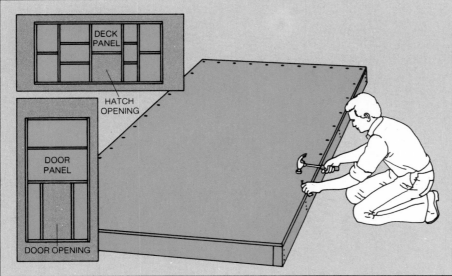

2 **Reinforcing the panels.** Spacing eightpenny nails about 6 inches apart, nail each plywood panel to a 4-by-8-foot frame consisting of four 2-by-4s, two of them 8 feet long and two 45 inches, set on edge and butt-nailed at the corners. Turn each panel and frame over and install three additional 45-inch 2-by-4 braces—spaced every 2 feet—along each wall panel lacking a door opening. To reinforce the deck panel *(top inset)*, place a 45-inch 2-by-4 brace 1½ feet in from each end and center another on each side edge of the hatch opening. Then nail cross braces between these 2-by-4s, centering one on the hinge edge of the hatch opening. On the door panel *(bottom inset)*, center one 45-inch 2-by-4 brace on the top edge of the door opening, install a second one midway between it and the top of the panel, and center two vertical 2-by-4 braces on the side edges of the door opening.

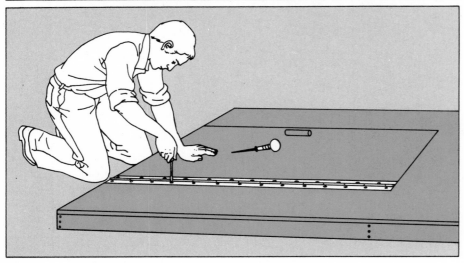

3 **Hinging the openings.** Use surface mounting to install stainless-steel or brass 1½-inch continuous hinges, often called piano hinges, to hang the door and hatch. Cut the hinges to the lengths needed with a hacksaw, leaving at least ¼ inch between the cut and the nearest screw hole. Position each hinge on its door or hatch. Make starter holes with an awl and drive ⅜-inch screws at the ends and in the middle of each hinge leaf. Swing the door or hatch to test for fit before driving the remaining screws.

Assembling the Playhouse

1 Anchoring the panels. Steady each panel against two 2-by-2 stakes, each 3½ feet long, that have been driven 1½ feet into the ground and positioned so they can be bolted to the panel's vertical framing pieces. Each stake should have two predrilled boltholes, at least 18 inches apart and with countersunk wells for nuts and washers on the outer side of the stake. Mark through the boltholes in each stake to match their positions on the panel. Drill boltholes through the panel frames at the marks, then secure the panels to their stakes with 4½-inch carriage bolts, their heads facing inward and the nuts countersunk into the stake (*inset*).

2 Bolting wall panels together. After anchoring the four wall panels to stakes as shown at left, drill boltholes—each having a countersunk well for the nut—at the back corners where the vertical panels meet a horizontal panel. (Omit the lower right corner since it is bolted to a stake.) Start the holes through the 2-by-4 framing of the horizontal panel and continue through the 2-by-4s that frame the upright panels—you will need an extension bit at least 8 inches long. Insert ⅜-inch carriage bolts, 5 inches long, heads facing inward, to secure the corners. To prepare for installing the upper deck, nail a 4-foot-long 2-by-4 across the inside frame of each vertical panel. Position it so that its top edge is flush with the top edge of the horizontal panels.

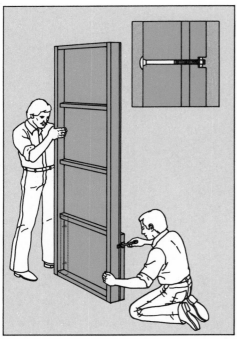

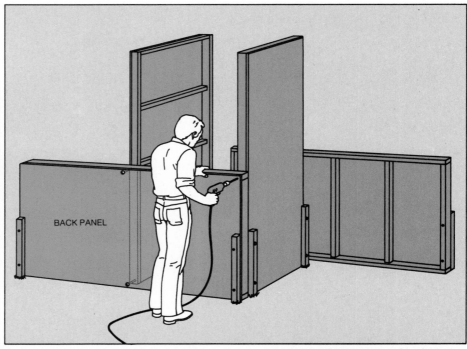

3 Installing the deck panel. Lift the deck panel into position over the 2-by-4 supports and center it so that it extends an equal distance beyond each horizontal wall panel. At each point where a wall-panel frame meets a deck-panel frame, drill holes and bolt the two together with ⅜-inch carriage bolts. Install eight bolts: Insert four, 5 inches long, through the edges of the upright-panel framing with the nuts countersunk on the outside, and four, 5½ inches long, down through the edges of the deck framing and the sides of the horizontal-panel framing, with the nuts countersunk underneath.

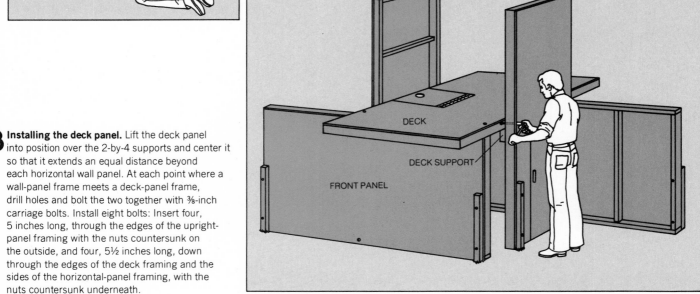

BACK PANEL

DECK

DECK SUPPORT

FRONT PANEL

Roofing the Second Story

Installing roof supports and rafters. On the upper deck, position a 4-by-4 roof-support post against the framing at each side of each vertical panel and toenail the bottom of each post to the deck framing. The two posts that stand against the rear panel should extend 1 foot above the top of the panel; the two for the front should be flush with the top of the panel.

When all the posts are secured, cut two 2-by-4s, each 4 feet long, and nail one across the tops of each pair of 4-by-4 posts.

Cut four 2-by-4s to serve as rafters between the 4-by-4 post assemblies. Position them on edge, spaced 16 inches on center, and toenail their ends to the tops of the roof-support frames. Cut a piece of ⅜-inch plywood for the roof and nail it to the tops of the rafters.

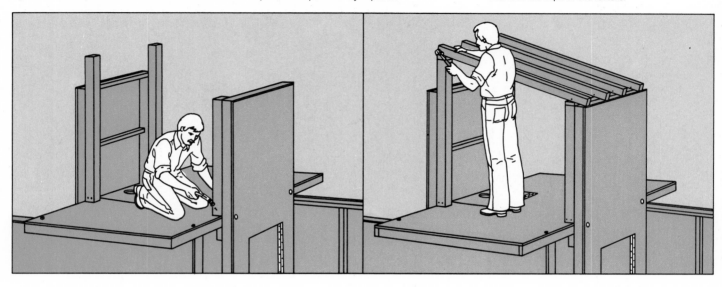

A Safety Railing around the Deck

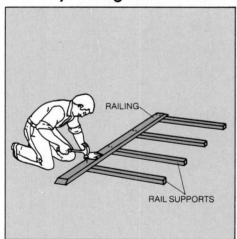

1 Assembling the railings. Preassemble railing sections on the ground by nailing 2-by-2 rails, 30 inches long, to a 2-by-4 stringer. On each deck end, cut the stringer 4 feet long, miter both ends, and space the rails evenly along it, conforming to local building codes. For each short side of the deck, cut a 1½-foot stringer with one mitered end and space three rails evenly across it. Have a helper steady the sections while you drill two holes for lag bolts through the bottom end of each rail and the frame of the deck. Space boltholes 1½ inches apart and make the bottom hole 1 inch from the bottom end of the rail.

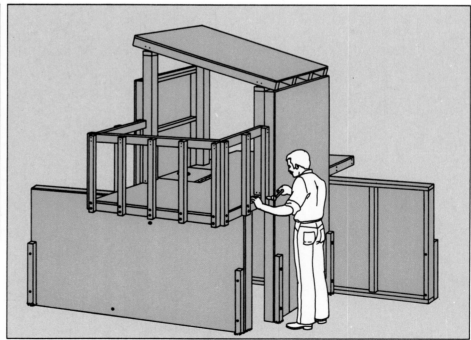

2 Installing the railing sections. Hold the preassembled railing sections in position and bolt the sections to the deck framing with ⅜-inch lag bolts. Join the mitered corners by driving finishing nails diagonally through from the top.

Offbeat Approaches to Child's Play

Everyone knows that children are more imaginative than adults but sometimes their elders give them stiff competition. The play structures shown here—some of them designed and built by parents, others by professionals—are ingenious, offbeat and in several instances handsome enough to remain in place as abstract sculptures long after the children have ceased to use them for play. At the same time, they offer their youthful occupants plenty of latitude for what psychologists call exploring their motor and cognitive skills—in other words, learning by doing.

Unlike run-of-the-mill metal swings and makeshift packing-crate playhouses, these play structures are solidly made of materials that weather beautifully—redwood, cedar, the scavenged beams and siding of old farm buildings. On those that are painted, the colors are bold primaries—like the splash of color visible through the door of the sentry-box tree house at right, which pays homage, in its color scheme, to the brilliant canvases of the painter Frank Stella.

Although clearly inspired by the clean lines and uncomplicated surfaces of modern design, several of these structures are far from simple in purpose. The massive assemblage of 10-by-10 timbers on page 79 is one element of a bristling construction described by its owner as "an attractive porcupine," which incorporates facilities for climbing, swinging and sliding. In summer, the central of the three climbing towers on page 80 turns into a fountain, spraying jets of water from holes in a hidden pipe that runs up the side of the tower. And the sleeping loft on page 75 is actually an afterthought, tucked between the tripod legs of a working windmill.

The amounts of time and money spent on these play structures also vary widely. Scrap lumber and "two afternoons and an evening" produced the biplane swing on page 78, which was made by a father whose hobby is woodworking. But a pair of professional carpenters worked four weeks on the climbing gym on page 78, to make the structure as durable and as safe as possible—which is why it cost between $1,000 and $2,000.

Crow's nest. Resting in the crotch of a live oak tree, 12 feet above the ground, this sentry-box tree house is well placed for surveying a child's world. The house sits on a triangular platform bracketed by a solid rail on the outward-facing side, and all of the exterior surfaces have been stained to blend in with the gray-green of the tree. The ladder-like steps mounting the trunk lead to a second arboreal dwelling for adults, about 15 feet higher up. The steps are fastened on with nails but, the owners observe, a few nails driven into a tree will not hurt it.

Two Aerial Hideaways and a Western Fort

Playhouses come in all sizes and shapes and need not conform to standard notions of what such structures should be. Of the three designs shown here, one is a treeborne A-frame whose hinged sides open up like the flaps of a tent; the second is a replica of a Western stockade, including an iron hitching ring beside the gate; and the third is a playful adjunct to the working windmill that provides electricity for the family's house nearby.

A shingled tent. Suspended from the apex of a triangular frame and supported by two 2-by-6 beams slung between twin trees, this A-frame is only an arm's length from the ground, but looks higher. It creaks romantically in the wind but is very sturdy, kept so by a wooden wedge that stabilizes the distance between the trees.

A recycled fort. Built from salvaged lumber that has aged to silver-gray, this stockade 6 feet high has a raised platform within and boasts a 14-foot lookout tower. The gate is bolted from the inside in traditional Old West fashion, and there is a secret back door for sneak attacks.

A sleeping loft aloft. The lower two thirds of this purposeful windmill contains what the owner calls a corncrib of wooden slats. It houses a triangular sleeping loft for his children, accessible by a ladder from a lower deck that the family uses as a gazebo on summer evenings.

A Fanciful Pegboard for Serious Play

Originally conceived as a tool for teaching nursery-school children to recognize abstract spatial concepts, this giant pegboard easily slides from its primary purpose into make-believe. It consists of a platform made of two layers of ¾-inch plywood with a frame of 2-by-6s sandwiched between them. Holes are drilled through the platform in both random and regular patterns to accept the ends of painted dowels that are from 2 feet to 4½ feet tall.

Some of the pegboard's holes are color-coded so that they will outline various simple shapes—circles, triangles, squares—when dowels are inserted in them. This is the pegboard's teaching mode. But the holes and dowels also adapt to the kind of pure play shown in the pictures on these pages. The young builders here are 4-year-olds, and their additional materials consist of a white bed sheet, a few painted cardboard boxes and some plastic flowers.

Alfresco dining. Eleven friends sit down to lunch in an airy pavilion they built for themselves by draping a sheet over randomly placed dowels.

Indoor gardening. A budding horticulturist erects a bed-sheet greenhouse over a row of plastic chrysanthemums that are ''planted'' in dowels wrapped with tape.

Queen for a day. Three cardboard boxes atilt on colorful dowels create a royal canopy over a child perched on a cardboard-box throne.

Invitations to Indulge in Youthful Acrobatics

The parents of children who lack a low-branched tree, with its natural facilities for swinging and climbing, can find any number of ingenious substitutes.

The three shown here include a plane that glides back and forth just above the ground, inviting youthful wingwalkers; a multipurpose gym that fits a slide, a swing, a climbing rope and dozens of climbing bars into the tight confines of an urban backyard; and the climbing section of a massive play gym that rises from the sand at water's edge like the bleached bones of an ancient shipwreck.

Plane for joyriding. Suspended from three points by plastic-coated steel cables, this bright-red biplane was made from scrap plywood. The struts are aluminum curtain tracks and the landing gear, scrap tricycle wheels.

Versatile gym. Designed for hard use, this redwood-and-cedar structure is constructed of the sturdiest, most durable materials firmly bolted together. The top deck is equipped with a weatherproof blackboard.

Seaside sculpture. Solidly made of 10-by-10 timbers, this climbing structure by the sea has survived harsh winter storms as well as the rough play of children

Climbing towers. Three wooden columns are lathe-cut or fitted with dowel steps at intervals wide enough to discourage younger children from climbing too high.

Synthetic Surfaces to Stretch the Seasons

In times past, ice skating was a winter sport and baseball was traditionally a summer activity. But today many seasonal sports no longer depend on the vagaries of the weather. Skaters can glide across interlocking squares of polymer-plastic ice. Downhill skiers in snowless parts of the South practice parallel turns on a white, slippery grass-like surface that may be covered with thousands of polyethylene pellets, or ski down slopes of white plastic bristles. Football teams play on artificial grass that is forever green.

These artificial surfaces are expensive, and none is common in backyards. But the products exist and may someday be within the reach of any homeowner.

Plastic ice was first manufactured in 1974 by a St. Louis firm, Skate On. The product consists of 2-foot squares of polymer plastic that are identically notched and fit together like pieces of a jigsaw puzzle. The squares are ¼ inch thick, weigh about 4 pounds each, and come in indoor or outdoor versions— the outdoor version withstands winter cold and glaring sun. The ice is available in red and blue, as well as white, and can be laid over any smooth, hard surface. It is portable, which has made it convenient for skating exhibitions on TV specials or at summer resorts.

However, the material has certain maintenance requirements. It needs to be treated daily with a special cleanser and a conditioner that creates a skating surface similar to that of real ice. Even with the conditioner, the plastic surface is about 10 per cent slower than real ice, and cannot be used for maneuvers that require long continuous glides, such as figure 8s. The material is also a sizable investment. Although less expensive than many other artificial surfaces, a 15-by-24-foot area of Skate On would cost about one fourth as much as an in-ground swimming pool.

For skiers, there are several snow substitutes, usable on hills with a slope of 10° to 15° and a run of 30 to 60 feet. A firm in Toronto manufactures one such surface—rolls of simulated white grass, called Poly Snow, 50 feet long and 3 feet wide. Used with silicone sprayed right on the surface or on the bottoms of skis, Poly Snow still remains about 10 per cent slower than real snow.

Poly Snow is frequently used on badly trampled areas around ski lifts. It was installed for this purpose in the staging areas for the 70-meter and 90-meter jump events at the 1980 Winter Olympics at Lake Placid, New York. When used on outdoor slopes, it is generally sprayed with tiny polyethylene beads that give the surface the consistency and behavior of a good powder snow. But Poly Snow is unlikely to be used in backyards for some time to come. Its cost is two to three times that of plastic ice, and it must be sprayed with silicone every two months.

Another artificial snow, called Pro-Snow, is produced by a California firm and resembles a honeycomb of 1¼-inch circles with bristles of various heights rising from their circumferences. The longest bristles are 1½ inches high. The varying lengths of the bristles give skiers improved downhill momentum as well as allowing them to carve good turns. The material, which costs about as much as Poly Snow, is manufactured both in 11-inch squares that snap together, and in 8-by-40-foot rolls.

As with real snow, the surface of Pro-Snow is faster in the morning and evening, when temperatures are lower, because the bristles are stiffer. However, spraying the surface with water before each use increases its speed.

Like avid skiers in search of year-round snow, other athletes crave a year-round turf. Artificial turf, which was originally developed for domed stadiums where real grass will not grow, is often called by one of its trade names, Astroturf. It is being used increasingly for outdoor playing fields. In addition to providing a mud-free surface that can be played on in the rain, it can be used 10 to 12 hours a day, which would destroy natural grass.

Ostensibly carefree—it does not need mowing, fertilizing or watering—artificial grass nevertheless needs maintenance. Like any carpeting material, it must be vacuumed and washed. Also, like other artificial surfaces, artificial grass does not behave exactly like the real McCoy. On a hot day, when the thermometer registers 90°, the temperature of an artificial-grass field may climb as high as 140° to 160°, unless it is cooled with water. Despite this problem for players, the durability and versatility of artificial turf will no doubt continue to bring an expansion of its use.

A Backyard Gym with a Variety of Attractions

Tarzan developed his muscles and his co-ordination skills in the jungle, climbing trees and swinging on vines. Your children can have the same fun and physical challenge right in your own backyard on a wood-and-steel play structure. By designing and building such a structure yourself, you can tailor it to the specific ages and needs of your family. At the same time, you save money—prefabricated kits are quite expensive.

Thoughtful planning and layout of any play area are essential to its success. First you must choose the kinds and sizes of equipment suitable—in terms of both challenge and safety—to the ages of the children who will use it. A simple swinging wooden bridge, for example, set 3 to 4 feet off the ground, will thrill a small child, while for older children with greater physical skills an 8-foot-high cargo net—available at marine-supply stores—will be more appealing. Sliding boards and fireman's poles that descend from an 8-foot height are reasonably safe for children 10 years old, but you should give younger children a 4- to 6-foot descent.

Generally the most successful play structures combine several activities—swinging, sliding and climbing, for example—in one interconnected unit. So experiment on paper with different arrangements of slides, swings, nets and ladders around one or more central platforms. Be sure to provide more than one access route to each platform, for variety and to handle the traffic. And in positioning the structure, remember to include enough ground space around it to balance its height; the area should extend out from the structure for a distance equal to half the structure's height.

Certain safety features never vary, regardless of the arrangement of the unit's parts. All platforms should have guardrails; all sharp corners should be rounded and smoothed with a power sander or a sanding attachment on an electric drill; all exposed bolt ends should be recessed in counterbored wells.

For stability, set each support post in a concrete footing. Cover the ground of the whole play area with a 6-inch layer of tanbark or shredded hardwood mulch;

dig to increase this to a depth of 1 foot at the bottom of a sliding board or fireman's pole. (For added protection, never end any sliding board less than 18 inches from the ground.) As a boundary for this mulch, you can use railroad ties or garden timbers, if they are treated with salt instead of toxic creosote. Otherwise, use 2-by-6 boards secured to stakes.

Once you have determined the design of your play structure, draw a detailed plan of it, including dimensions of all its parts—heights, lengths, widths. Then compose a shopping list. For all wooden parts use cedar, redwood or pressure-treated pine; the first two are attractive but are more expensive. Use 4-by-4s for posts, buying vertical posts 3 feet longer than their ultimate height, to allow for setting them in the ground. For the platform headers and decking, you will need 2-by-6 lumber; for the sliding board, 2-by-8s and a panel of ¾-inch plywood; for the seesaw and sandbox, 2-by-10s.

Besides wood, the other material you will need in quantity is galvanized-steel pipe with a 1-inch outside diameter for ladder rungs and guardrails. The pipes should be threaded on each end to accept flanges, and long enough to span the distance between support posts and go through the wood and the flanges mounted on the outsides of the posts.

Depending on the dimensions of your design, these lengths of pipe may have to be cut and threaded to order. Many plumbing-supply companies or hardware stores will cut and thread at a cost only slightly higher than that of prethreaded standard-length pipe, but check this locally. If standard lengths are appreciably cheaper, it would make sense to tailor your design to their dimensions.

Other plumbing supplies you will need include caps to seal pipe ends. If your plan includes a fireman's pole, you will also need three pieces of 3-inch pipe, two 90° elbow connections and a flange to anchor the pipe to the platform.

Most of the hardware needed for joining the components shown here is available at hardware stores. To join the wooden parts, use ½-inch carriage bolts, because their smooth, round heads make

them safer for children than square-headed machine bolts. Wherever you will countersink nuts below the surface of the wood, the length of the bolt shank should equal the thickness of the wood parts it will secure; where the shank can safely project, it should be ½ inch longer. To fasten the chains to the swing, and the cargo net to the platform, you will need ½-inch-thick eyebolts whose length is decided the same way—and to use with the eyebolts, 1½- to 2-inch washers. For the swing, you will also need a heavy-duty ½-inch steel swivel and three overlapping hooks of the same gauge.

The chains used for the tire swing and the swinging bridge should have links of a type called proof coil, invisibly welded to produce smooth seams. The link width for swing chains should be ½ inch, for bridge chains ¾ inch. To fasten the chains of the swinging bridge to their support posts, you will need saddle clamps and 8-inch lengths of galvanized-steel rod that fit through the links. Finally, you will need a roll of .016-inch aluminum flashing, to cover the sliding board.

The first step in constructing the play structure is to plot the positions for the basic support posts. Set these posts into concrete footings 2½ feet deep *(pages 50-51)* and attach headers for the platforms from which the various components will radiate. All the techniques needed for assembling the platforms and the components are shown on the following pages—except for hanging the cargo net, whose corners are simply tied to eyebolts in four support posts. For guardrails and access ladders, added when all other components are in place, pipes are attached to support posts with flanges, just as they are to the sides of an overhead ladder *(page 85, bottom)*.

Periodically inspect the play structure for safety. Check nuts for loosening (which you can forestall somewhat with a spray compound that freezes them in place, available at hardware stores). Keep mulch evenly distributed, particularly around seesaws, sliding boards and fireman's poles. Make sure the deck screws for poles are tight; inspect swing hardware regularly and replace worn parts.

Anatomy of a play area. This play area represents one of many possible configurations. The nucleus of the structure is two 4-by-6 platforms—one 8 feet high and one 4 feet high—connected by a horizontal overhead ladder. The 2-by-6 floorboards for each platform are supported by two pairs of 2-by-6 headers that are bolted to 4-by-4 corner posts. These posts—which are set in concrete to a depth of 2½ feet—also extend 3 feet above the level of the platform. Lengths of 1-inch pipe serve as guardrails on all the open sides of the platforms and as rungs for the vertical and overhead ladders.

An aluminum-covered sliding board, a fireman's pole and a cargo net for climbing radiate from three sides of the 8-foot-high platform. Additional 4-by-4 posts, set beyond the 4-foot-high platform, provide for the installation of the tire swing and the swinging bridge. Off to one side of the structure, away from the main flow of traffic, is a seesaw, and on the other side is a sandbox. A 6-inch layer of shredded hardwood mulch covers the entire play area to cushion any falls.

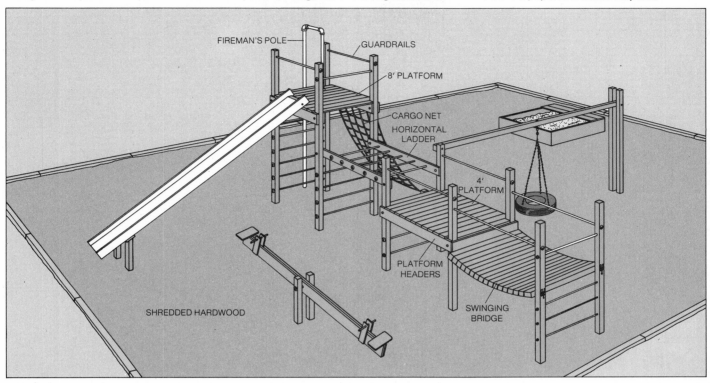

FIREMAN'S POLE

GUARDRAILS

8' PLATFORM

CARGO NET

HORIZONTAL LADDER

4' PLATFORM

PLATFORM HEADERS

SHREDDED HARDWOOD

SWINGING BRIDGE

Building a Basic Platform

1 Predrilling posts and headers. At a point 4¼ inches below the final platform height, drill a ½-inch hole through the center of one corner post for the platform, making sure—if your platform is rectangular—to drill the hole through the post face on the rectangle's long side. Cut four 2-by-6 headers the length of the rectangle's long side, and mark the headers' center lines by snapping a chalk line from end to end (it is easier to do this while resting the headers on sawhorses). Mark points on the center lines 1¾ inches from each end of the headers and drill a ½-inch hole at each of the marks.

2 **Installing the platform headers.** Align a predrilled hole in one header with the predrilled hole on the post. Slip a bolt through the two and, while a helper holds the header level, mark the position of the predrilled hole at the other end of the header on the post behind it. Lower the header, drill a ½-inch hole through the post at the mark, then slip a bolt through both holes, as above. Add a second header to the same bolts on the insides of the two posts, sandwiching the posts between the headers.

To find the corresponding position for the headers at the opposite side of the platform, hold a board level on top of the assembled headers and extend it across to each of the opposite posts in turn. Pencil this height on the post. Then mark and drill the holes in the posts, and bolt the headers in place, as above.

3 **Adding the deck.** Working in tandem with a helper on the far side of the platform, lay 2-by-6 deck boards—cut to fit flush with the edges of the outer headers—across the platform area, and nail them in place. Space the boards ¼ inch apart for drainage and drive nails through the boards into all four headers, centering the nails in the header edges. Rip the last board lengthwise, if necessary, to fit it into the remaining space. Then, to complete the platform, cut two additional 2-by-4 deck boards to fit between the corner posts, rest them on the inner headers and nail them in place.

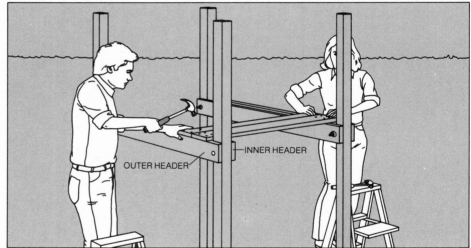

INNER HEADER

OUTER HEADER

A Swinging Jungle Bridge

1 **Stringing the pieces together.** Thread a length of chain with ¾-inch-wide links through ⅞-inch holes predrilled through a series of 4-by-4s, 6 inches in from each end. The 4-by-4s should be cut 15½ inches longer than the space between end posts, and the chains should be long enough to allow 1 inch of sag for every foot of span, plus 2 feet for fastening the ends. To find the number of 4-by-4s needed, measure the distance the bridge will span in inches and divide this by 3½; to this number of 4-by-4s, add two more, to allow for sag.

Drill ⅞-inch installation holes, at identical heights, through all support posts. At the platform end, pull each chain through its installation hole, slip an 8-inch galvanized-steel rod through a link of each chain to hold it, and secure the rod to the post with two saddle clamps (inset).

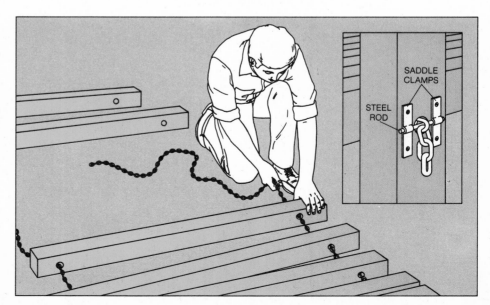

SADDLE CLAMPS

STEEL ROD

2 Hanging the bridge. Tie about 3 feet of nylon cord to the unattached ends of the chains, thread the cords through the installation holes in the second pair of support posts and, working with a helper, hoist the bridge off the ground by pulling on the cords. Pull until the last 4-by-4 is against the outer support posts, then secure the ends of the chains with steel rods and saddle clamps as on the platform posts.

Hand-over-Hand on a Horizontal Ladder

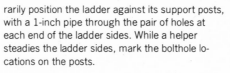

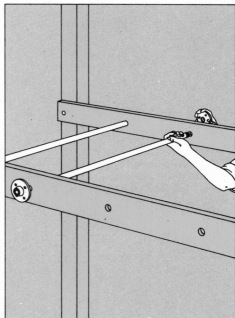

1 Marking the ladder sides. Cut two 2-by-6 boards long enough to span and overlap the supporting posts for the ladder, snap a chalk line to mark their lengthwise centers and mark points on the line for boltholes, 1¾ inch in from each end. Between the bolt marks, measure off 1-foot intervals for rungs. Set the boards on sawhorses and drill ½-inch holes for the bolts and 1-inch holes for the rungs, centering the holes over the crossed lines marking their positions. Tempo-

rarily position the ladder against its support posts, with a 1-inch pipe through the pair of holes at each end of the ladder sides. While a helper steadies the ladder sides, mark the bolthole locations on the posts.

Drill ½-inch holes through the posts at these marks. Slip a carriage bolt through the ladder sides and the posts, bolthead facing the inside of the ladder, and fasten in place.

2 Fastening the pipe rungs. After you have bolted the ladder sides to their support posts (with all of the bolt ends in countersunk wells), screw a threaded flange onto one end of a threaded pipe. Slide the pipe through a pair of rung holes, anchoring it by screwing a second flange onto the end on the opposite side of the ladder. Repeat for the remaining rungs, then screw all of the flanges securely into place against the ladder sides, using 1-inch wood screws.

A Sliding Board Made of Wood and Aluminum

1 Calculating the slide length. With a helper holding one end, stretch a measuring tape from the edge of the platform where you will install the slide to a stake driven into the ground at a distance from the platform that equals 1½ times its height. Add 2 feet to this measurement to get the final slide length. For the sliding surface, cut two strips of ¾-inch plywood, each 2 feet wide, with a combined length equal to the final slide length. Then cut two 2-by-8 side boards long enough to extend 3 inches beyond the final slide length. Round all the sharp corners.

2 Joining the plywood strips. Lay the 2-foot-wide plywood strips on the ground end to end and slide two 2-by-6 braces, each a foot long, underneath the strips where they meet. Position the braces so they are perpendicular to, and centered on, the joint between strips. Use extra 2-by-6 scraps as supports at the outer ends to keep the strips level while you drive 1¾-inch wood screws through the plywood into the braces to secure the joint and form a continuous slide.

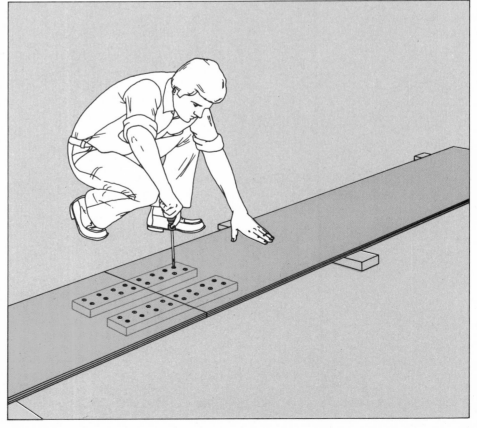

3 **Covering the slide with aluminum.** Wrap each
side board in a strip of .016-inch aluminum
flashing 21 inches wide and 3 inches longer than
the board. Position the board on the flashing
so that when wrapping is complete, the exposed
edge of flashing will fall on the inner face of
the board, cut edge down, about 2 inches in from
what will be the board's lower edge; thus the
sharp edge of the flashing will eventually be hidden under the plywood base of the slide. Make
sure the flashing overlaps the ends of the boards
equally, 1½ inches at each end.

Begin the lengthwise wrapping procedure by
securing the first edge of the flashing with 1-inch
roofing nails at 1-foot intervals along the entire
board. Fold the second edge over the first and repeat the nailing procedure. Then fold the ends
of the flashing over the board ends as you would
finish wrapping a package, folding in first the
bottom edge, then the top edge, then the outer
face and finally the inner face (inset). Secure the
wrapped ends with roofing nails.

To cover the plywood base, cut a strip of flashing
large enough to overlap the top, bottom and
side edges of the base by 6 inches; fold and nail
the aluminum to the underside of the base, working on the ends first, then the sides.

4 **Assembling the slide pieces.** Lay the aluminum-
covered plywood base upside down, resting it
on supports that lift it at least 4 inches off the
ground. Secure the side boards to the plywood
edges with 3-inch steel angle irons, first fastening
the angle irons along the side boards at intervals of 1½ feet with 1½-inch wood screws, setting
the end of one leg of each iron flush with the
lower edge of the board (inset). When all the angle irons have been secured, place the side
boards against the base so that the side boards
are flush with the base at one end and extend
3 inches beyond it at the other end; fasten the
second leg of each iron to the underside of the
base with ¾-inch wood screws.

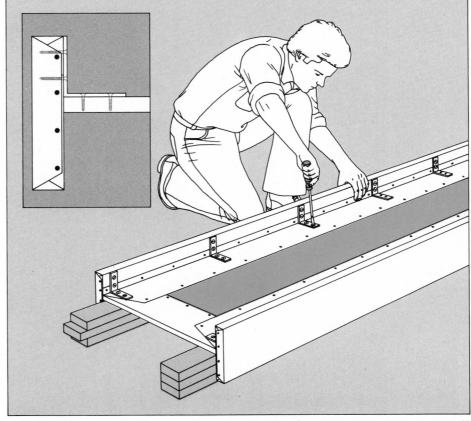

5 **Adding a top support.** On the edge of the platform chosen for the slide, mount a 4-by-4 support
2 feet long, by driving ½-inch lag bolts, 4½
inches long, through two predrilled holes that
have countersunk wells ½ inch deep for the
boltheads *(inset)*. Position the slide support exactly flush with the edge of the deck, and plot the
bolt locations to fall in the centers of deck boards.

6 **Fastening the slide to the platform.** Rest the
top end of the slide's plywood base—the end with
the 3-inch side-board extensions—bracketing the
ends of the 4-by-4 support. As a helper holds
the bottom end of the slide steady on three
stacked cinder blocks, drill a ½-inch hole through
each side-board extension and 2 inches into
the ends of the 4-by-4. Drive ½-inch lag bolts,
5 inches long, through the holes into the ends of
the 4-by-4, but do not tighten them completely.

7 **Marking and cutting support posts.** With the bottom end of the slide base still resting on the stacked cinder blocks, have a helper hold a 6-foot length of 4-by-4 plumb against a side board, 18 inches up from the slide's bottom end. Reach under the slide and mark the angle of the side board on the 4-by-4. At the same time mark the location where the 4-by-4 touches the ground, as a guide for a posthole. Use a T bevel to copy the marked angle at a point 3 feet higher up the post *(inset)* and cut the post along this second line. Similarly mark and cut the second support post and indicate the position of its posthole.

Join the support posts across their angled tops with a piece of 2-by-10 lumber, 2 feet 3 inches long, positioning the 2-by-10 so that its ends are flush with the outer faces of the two posts, and centering the post ends on the face of the 2-by-10. Dig footing holes 2½ feet deep for both support posts. You can, if necessary, loosen the top bolts and raise the bottom of the slide temporarily, propping it on a stepladder; but leave the cinder blocks in place.

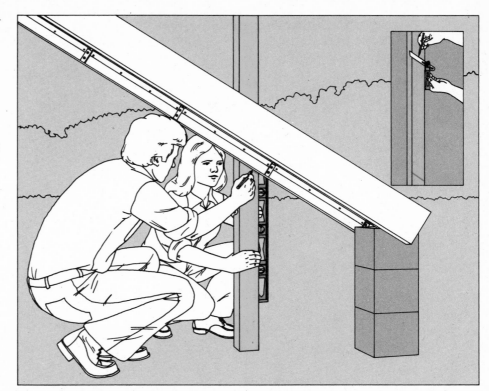

8 **Nailing the support posts to the slide.** With the slide bottom resting on the cinder blocks and while a helper steadies the support-post assembly, shimmed if necessary in its footing holes, drive nails up through the 2-by-10 crosspiece into the edges of the side boards. Make sure the ends of the 2-by-10 crosspiece are flush with the outside faces of the side boards, and use two eightpenny nails at each corner. Then tighten the lag bolts at the top of the slide.

Pour concrete to fill the footing holes around the posts *(page 51)*. Leave the cinder blocks in place to support the end of the slide until the cement has set. Once it has set, remove the cinder blocks and dig a hole 4 feet square and 6 inches deep at the base of the slide. Fill the hole with extra mulch to serve as a cushion.

Swinging and Swiveling on a Tire

1 Preparing the tire. Push 4-inch eyebolts down through three ½-inch holes that have been pre-drilled at equal distances around one side of a tire. Fasten the eyebolts in place by slipping a screwdriver shaft through each eye to steady it while you reach inside the tire, slide a 1½-inch washer over the bolt shank and screw on a nut (*inset*). Tighten the nuts with pliers.

2 Hooking the chains to the eyebolts. Slip a ½-inch-thick overlapping hook through each eyebolt, slip the last link of a length of chain onto each hook, and close the overlapping sections of the hook with channel-joint pliers. Make sure the chains are of equal length, and are long enough to let the swing hang the correct distance from the ground—at least 2 feet.

3 Hanging the swing. Attach the three tire chains to the previously assembled overhead hardware while a helper holds the tire so that the chains are slightly slack. For the overhead hardware, drill a hole and run a ½-inch-thick eyebolt 6 inches long through an overhead support beam and fasten it at the top of the beam with a washer and bolt. Connect the eyebolt to the top loop of a ½-inch swivel by means of a ½-inch overlapping hook, pinching the ends of the hook together with channel-joint pliers. Then connect the tire chains to the bottom loop of the swivel with a second overlapping hook.

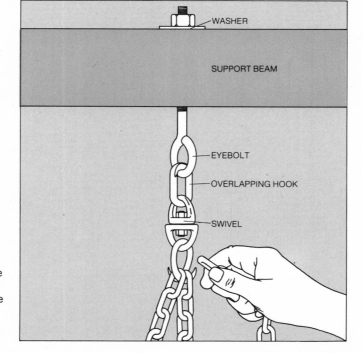

WASHER

SUPPORT BEAM

EYEBOLT

OVERLAPPING HOOK

SWIVEL

A Fireman's Pole to Slide On

1 **Fitting the pipes together.** Assemble a U-shaped fireman's pole from 3-inch pipe, using a plumber's wrench and wrapping the pipe beneath the wrench with a rag to protect the metal from abrasion. Using scrap lengths of 4-by-4 lumber as supports, first screw a 90° elbow onto a length of pipe that is 7 feet longer than the distance from the ground to the top of the platform. Screw a length of pipe 2 feet long to the other end of the elbow and add a second 90° elbow to the opposite end of the 2-foot pipe. Then add a third length of pipe, 4 feet long, to the opposite end of the second elbow. Screw a flange to the free end of this 4-foot pipe.

2 **Setting the pole in place.** While a helper on the ground steadies the bottom of the long pole in a footing hole 2½ feet deep and 1 foot away from the platform, swing the top of the pole until the flange is centered over a deck board and mark the positions of the screw holes for attaching the flange. Drill starter holes at the marks and screw the flange to the deck, using 1½-inch No. 10 wood screws. Plumb the slide pole with a level—bracing it with 2-by-4s if necessary—then secure it by pouring concrete (*page 51*) to fill its footing hole.

Note: If you are constructing the fireman's pole on a side of the structure that also contains access rungs, position the pole to one side of the platform to allow one child to use the pole while another climbs the rungs.

Sandbox with a Plastic Liner

Lining the frame and adding a seat. Into a simple square frame made by butt-nailing together the ends of four 2-by-10s, staple a bottom of 2-mil plastic sheeting 1 foot larger than the dimensions of the frame. Push the plastic flat against the ground and the box sides, and staple at 6-inch intervals, folding the plastic neatly at the corners of the box.

Add a seat at one end of the sandbox by nailing two 2-by-6s to the edges of the sandbox frame, spacing them ¼ inch apart. Pour sand into the box to a level about 2 inches from the top. Make a removable cover that a child can slide over the sandbox when it is not in use—in this example *(inset)*, two pieces of thin plywood hinged at the center for easy handling.

Assembling a Seesaw

1 Preparing the spine. Stack two 2-by-10 boards, each 10 feet long; working on a flat surface, nail them together with eightpenny nails in a zigzag pattern. Drill a 1-inch hole through the exact center of the board assembly, 5 feet from each end and 4¾ inches from each edge.

For support posts, use two 4-by-4s, each 5 feet long, set 2½ feet deep in concrete footings *(page 51)* and spaced 3½ inches apart.

2 **Installing handholds and seats.** Construct a mounting for each of two handholds from two 2-by-6 boards, 14 inches long; round all the corners and predrill 1-inch dowel holes for the handholds. Center the dowel holes 3 inches in from the ends of the mounting boards. To assemble, screw one mounting board to one side of the spine, 18 inches from the end; slip a dowel, 1 inch in diameter and 20 inches long, through it and slide the second mounting board over the dowel from the other side of the spine. Adjust the dowel until it is level, then screw the second mounting board in place. Drive a 16-penny nail down through the top edge of each mounting board into the dowel.

To make seats *(inset)*, round the corners of two 2-by-10s, each 12 inches long, center one across each end of the spine 8 inches behind a handhold, and nail through the seats into the top edge of the spine. Then turn the seesaw over and, resting it on sawhorses, anchor the seats to the spine with angle irons and screws, using four angle irons per seat, two on each side.

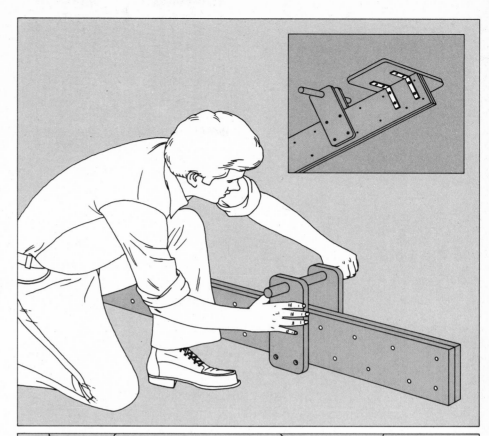

3 **Adding a pivot.** Drill a 1-inch hole through the center of each 4-by-4 seesaw support post, 6 inches down from the top. Line up the spine's center hole with the holes in the posts and slide an 11-inch-long piece of 1-inch pipe, threaded at both ends, through the three holes and anchor each end of the pipe to one of the support posts with a flange and 2-inch wood screws.

The Joys of Water, Cool or Hot

A secluded tub open to the sky. Seen through a circular entrance cut into a redwood screen, this 10-foot-wide hot tub combines the sybaritic pleasures of warm water and warm sun. The screen, rough-hewn planks of varying heights, 4½ to 8 feet tall, envelops not only the tub but a smooth cedar deck and a wide cedar staircase.

Water has always had an irresistible appeal; in fact, it was an object of worship long before it became a source of pleasure. Even before Aristotle described water as one of the four elements of the universe, the Greeks celebrated its sacred properties by assigning gods to springs, rivers and lakes. More recent societies have celebrated water's healing and cleansing powers; public baths thrived in the Roman Empire 2,000 years ago, as they do in Japan today. Moorish pools lined in stone or brick introduced the sight and sound of water, piped from afar, to desert gardens where it had never appeared naturally. And all over the world, rural ponds, used for watering livestock and irrigating crops, served also for bathing and fishing.

Modern construction techniques and materials make it possible for people to enjoy the pleasures of water at home for a tiny fraction of the labor and expense that were involved in building Roman baths or Moorish pools. Today's hot tubs, descendants of small Japanese baths, provide a place to relax taut muscles and nerves in soothing warmth. A swimming pool, bigger and cooler than a hot tub, comes into its own as the summer sun moves higher and swimmers can simultaneously escape the heat and enjoy invigorating exercise. A pond or lake displays other water joys: Such a body of water may provide opportunities for fishing and boating, as well as the simple pleasure of watching the passage of clouds and colors, reflected by the ever-changing surface of the water.

Whatever role you plan for water in your home recreation area, special structures can add to your enjoyment. Steps or a ladder provide access to a hot tub, and you can hide the heater and the plumbing with a fence. A deck or raised walk between tub and house will keep mud from being tracked into either. Around a swimming pool, too, a deck is a perfect adjunct—it offers an area for drying off, tanning, enjoying the sun and socializing. Piers and rafts give swimmers and boaters quick and convenient access to the waters of a lake.

Safety should be primary in your planning: For all its delights, water is unforgiving of carelessness. Make sure that unattended pools, ponds and hot tubs are not accessible to children; provide a fence for a pool or a cover for a hot tub. In many cases a pool can be positioned so that parents engaged in other activities can still keep an eye on the children when they are in the water. If everyone who uses such facilities understands the overriding importance of water safety and knows the basic rules, emergencies are unlikely to occur.

If the electrical equipment you are installing with a hot tub or swimming pool is not equipped with factory-installed protection against ground faults, add a lifesaving ground fault interrupter circuit breaker *(page 54)* to the electrical line serving the equipment.

How to Assemble and Install an Above-ground Pool

An above-ground pool, available in kit form and easily assembled with the help of some friends in two or three days, can provide years of swimming pleasure with a relatively small investment.

The most economical of these pools is circular, with a continuous wall of sheet aluminum or lightweight steel. However, a wall made of heavier interlocking metal panels is stronger and better suited to carrying part of the weight of walkways and decks, and an oblong pool (often called "oval" by manufacturers, but actually a rectangle with semicircular ends) provides more swimming space with relatively little extra installation effort.

When you choose a pool, consider the accessories available. Some manufacturers include a safety fence, required in most localities to prevent accidents in an unattended pool; you may want a fence that affords privacy as well as safety. Some manufacturers also sell decks as a package with their pools, or as optional add-ons for later installation. If your pool is to be part of an overall landscaping plan, you may prefer to build your own deck *(pages 107-111)*, designing it to link the pool with the house or with other areas of the yard.

In choosing the pool site, be sure that it will afford easy access to natural drainage or to storm sewers that can accommodate a large volume of water when you need to drain the pool. Provide for electricity to run the filter pump and plan the pump location. Then position the wall so that precut holes for filter connections will be convenient to it.

The pool site must be firm and level. A filled 20-foot circular pool weighs nearly 40 tons and even a tilt of as little as 1° is enough to throw a disproportionate amount of this weight against one wall. If your yard is already fairly level, you need only remove the sod until you reach solid earth. If the site slopes more than 4 inches overall, you will have to grade it roughly level *(page 14)* before beginning the fine grading that is part of the normal pool installation. Do not install the pool over filled land, or on soft or sandy soil, or on a site that is subject to heavy runoff after a rain.

In fine-grading the site, all the earth is removed above the level of the site's lowest point. For maximum wall strength, the grade variation at the pool's perimeter should not exceed an inch; some warranties are voided if this variation exceeds 2 inches. Inside the perimeter the grade is less critical, but variations should be less than 2 inches. To provide a smooth pool bottom and protect the pool liner from small stones and roots, the entire undersurface of the pool is covered with clean masonry sand, free of gravel. One ton of sand is enough for every 90 square feet of pool area.

When planning the installation, check the weather forecast. You will need at least three rain-free days to complete the work—and extensive earth-moving will require more time. Avoid setting up the wall on a windy day, because the unsupported wall can easily blow down; this could damage the wall and the bottom track, and gouge the smoothly graded surface. If the weather is cool, warm the pool liner by spreading it out on a sunny lawn for an hour or so, or unpack it and leave it in a warm room a few hours before installing it. Warming the liner will make the removal of wrinkles easier.

Precise Preparation of a Site

1 **Marking the pool perimeter.** For an oblong pool, drive two stakes into the ground to serve as reference points for plotting the pool's semicircular ends and its rectangular center. For dimensions, refer to the manufacturer's instructions.

Beginning with the central rectangle *(inset, near right)*, locate points A, B, C and D by laying out two lines the width of the pool, through the two reference stakes; the lines should be parallel, with their centers on the reference stakes. Connect the ends of the lines to form right angles at points A, B, C and D. You can check these angles by measuring the diagonals AD and CB, which should be identical in length. Mark the pool's sides by using a stick or a trowel blade to scribe a line in the ground from A to C and from B to D *(inset, near right)*. Scribe the pool's semicircular ends by pivoting a steel measuring tape on a nail driven into each reference stake, using half the pool's width as a radius.

For a circular pool *(inset, far right)*, similarly pivot a steel measuring tape around a stake you have driven to mark the pool's center.

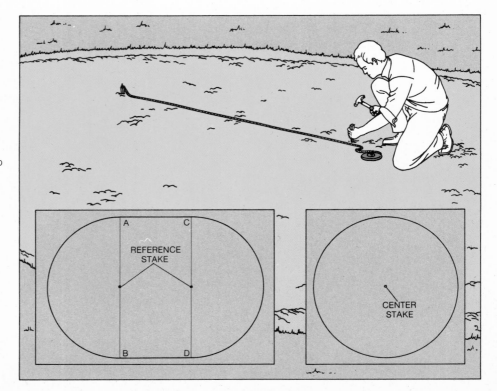

REFERENCE STAKE

CENTER STAKE

2 Making a radial level. To measure the grade at the pool's perimeter, make a radial level from a straight 2-by-4 by taping a carpenter's level to the edge of the 2-by-4 at one end and drilling a pivoting hole ¼ inch in diameter and 2 inches deep in the edge of the opposite end. To allow for later grading around the pool, the radial level for a circular pool should be about a foot longer than the radius of the pool and the distance from its pivoting hole to its outer end should be 6 inches greater than the pool's radius. For an oblong pool, the radial level should be about a foot longer than the distance from either reference stake (*Step 1*) to the center of the straight sides, and the distance from the level's pivoting hole to its outer end should be 6 inches greater than the radius of the pool's semicircular ends.

For a circular pool, pivot the radial level on a nail driven in the center stake. For an oblong pool, pivot the level on nails in the two reference stakes.

3 Finding the lowest spot. Holding a yardstick at the outer end of the radial level, and making sure the level is exactly horizontal, measure the distance from the level to the ground. Repeat this procedure in a swath 12 inches wide straddling the pool's perimeter, measuring every foot or so, to find the point where the distance from the level to the ground is greatest.

To find the low point in the straight sections of an oblong pool, drive the taller reference stake farther into the ground until its top is the same height as the other, as measured by a line level (*page 15*). Then, with the radial level off the pivot nails, slide the radial level along the top of one stake, measuring the distance to the ground at 1-foot intervals, continuing to the midpoint of each side. Repeat, using the reference stake at the other end of the pool.

When you have found the perimeter's lowest point, nail two 1-foot-long pieces of 2-by-4 to the underside of the radial level's outer end, positioning the blocks so that their midpoint falls on the perimeter of the pool (*Step 4, overleaf*). Put the level onto the pivot stake, rest the blocks on the ground at the lowest spot, and adjust the depth of the stake, raising it or lowering it until the radial level is exactly horizontal.

4 **Grading the perimeter.** Starting from the lowest point, swing the radial level around the perimeter, removing earth in a foot-wide swath with a trowel or a spade until the ground beneath the blocks is level (*below, left*). When you come to the straight sides of an oblong pool (*below, right*), take the radial level off the pivot nail and slide it across the top of each pivot stake as you did in establishing the perimeter's low point.

When the perimeter has been completely graded, remove enough earth within the perimeter so that no part of the pool area will have a variance of more than 2 inches in height from the perimeter grade. Dig out any protruding rocks and roots. When the entire pool area has been graded, pile sand inside the perimeter to be used later in smoothing the pool bottom.

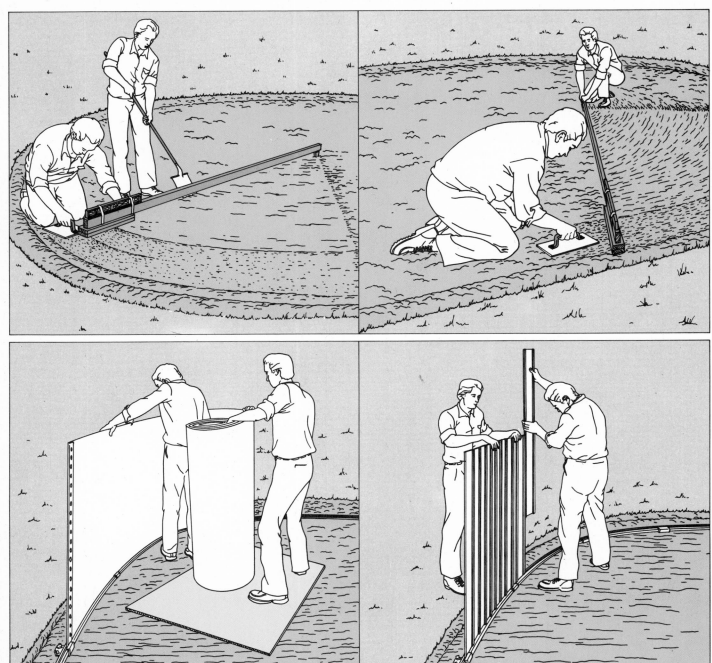

5 **Assembling the wall.** Place the bottom track for the wall around the graded perimeter, joining it according to the manufacturer's specifications. Insert the wall into the track. Protect the bottom of a continuous-sheet wall (*above, left*) as you unroll it by resting it on a piece of cardboard, tilting the roll slightly and sliding the cardboard along the track as you work.

If your pool has a panel wall (*above, right*), slip the panel joints together and slide the panels into the track. Have helpers hold the wall erect at several points until it is completely assembled and braced. Put the pool ladder in position over the wall for access to the working area. When the wall has been assembled, distribute sand evenly over the pool area and bank 2 inches of earth against the base of the outside wall.

Smoothing the Sand Bottom

1 Leveling the sand. Remove the blocks from the outer end of the radial level and rest the end of the level on the wall track. Then adjust the height of the pivot stake until the radial level is horizontal. Sweep the level slowly around the pool, removing high spots and filling in low points. Throw excess sand against the base of the wall, where it will be used to make a cove—a sloping surface that will help support the liner. Sprinkle the leveled sand with enough water to make it easy to pack together, then use a heavy tamper to pack it firm. When all the sand has been tamped, remove any remaining high and low areas by lightly sweeping the radial level one last time around the pool area. Then remove the level and its pivot stakes.

2 Building the cove. Using a concrete-finishing float, pack and smooth the sand against the wall into a slanting cove (*inset*) extending about 5 inches above the track and 7 inches away from the wall. Keep the dimensions of the cove consistent, adding more sand if needed.

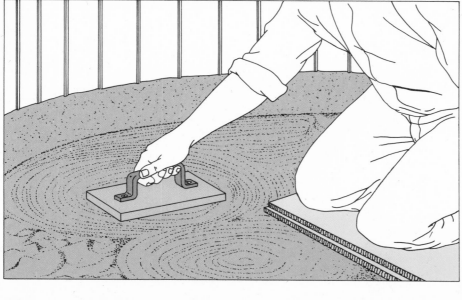

3 Smoothing the sand. Use the wooden float with a circular skimming motion to remove the last surface irregularities from the sand, first smoothing the cove and about a foot of the bottom adjacent to the cove, then working across the rest of the bottom so that you will end at the pool ladder. Place a doubled sheet of corrugated cardboard underneath you to keep your knees and toes from denting the packed sand. When you reach the ladder, place its base on another piece of cardboard laid over a smoothed area of sand and finish smoothing the bottom.

Installation of a Liner

1 **Spreading the liner.** While you and one helper lift the liner, folded accordion-style, over the wall and into the pool, have a second helper hold one edge of the liner so it overlaps the top of the wall. Working from this point around the outside of the pool, gradually lift and pull the liner edge over the top of the wall, using additional helpers to hold it in place as needed, until the entire liner overlaps the top of the wall. Fasten the liner in place temporarily with liner clamps provided with the pool.

If your liner snaps into a channel instead of overlapping the wall (*inset*), use the same procedure to spread the liner, working from one point and snapping the bead into the channel as you work around the pool's circumference.

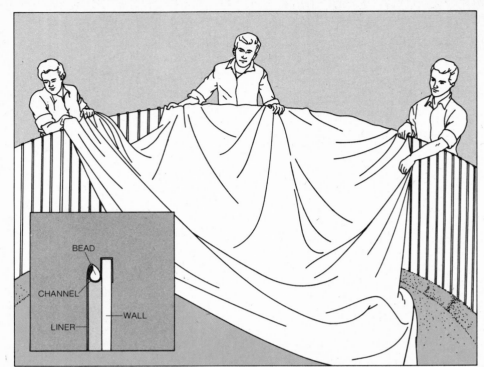

BEAD

CHANNEL

WALL

LINER

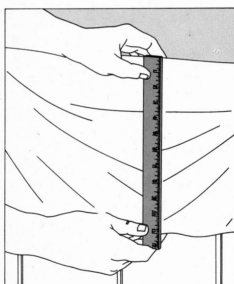

2 **Getting the edges even.** For a liner that overlaps the edge, adjust the overlap by unclamping the liner at one point and positioning it so that the bottom seam is even with the top of the sand cove; reclamp the liner and measure the amount of overlap. Gradually move around the wall, repositioning the rest of the liner overlap by the same amount. Then check the entire liner for proper fit: The liner is too tight if it draws away from the wall and floor; it is too loose if there are large folds of vinyl on the floor and wall. Correct the fit by uniformly increasing or decreasing the overlap; you may have to repeat this procedure several times to get the fit just right.

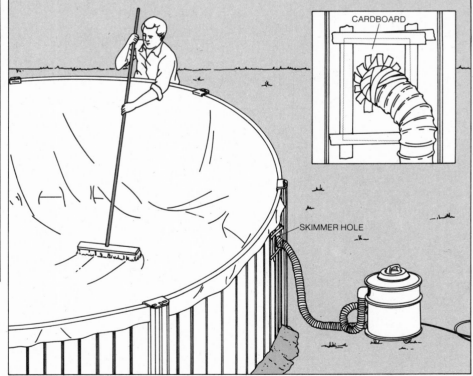

CARDBOARD

SKIMMER HOLE

3 **Smoothing the liner.** Run a vacuum-cleaner hose through the skimmer hole in the pool wall and down behind the liner, and use it to draw air from between the liner and the pool wall as you remove wrinkles. For a tight seal between the hose and the skimmer hole, use cardboard and masking tape (*inset*). Re-move wrinkles from the bottom by gently pushing the liner toward the wall with a pool-cleaning brush or a long-handled soft broom. Then work upward along the wall. When you have removed as many wrinkles as you can with the brush, turn off the vacuum cleaner and begin filling the pool with water.

4 **Removing the last wrinkles.** Put on your swim suit and, as the pool fills to a depth of 1 or 2 inches, get inside and pull out the remaining bottom wrinkles by grasping the liner in front of each wrinkle and pulling it toward the wall, then releasing the liner and repeating the action a few inches nearer to the wall. Kneel on a rubber floormat so that you do not dent the sand bottom. When all the wrinkles have been pulled over to the wall, get out of the pool and use the same procedure to pull the wrinkles up to the top of the wall. Unclamp the liner from the top of the wall, one section at a time, to draw these wrinkles over the top.

When you are satisfied with the smoothness of the liner, finish assembling the top of the wall according to the manufacturer's instructions.

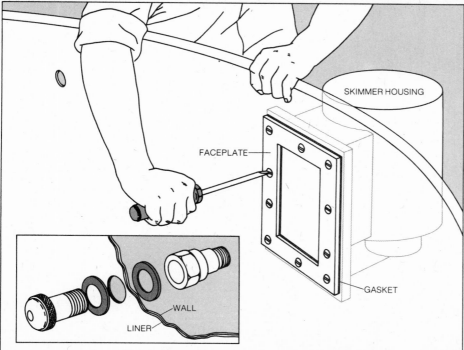

5 **Putting fittings through the liner.** Screw the skimmer faceplate and its gasket into place on the inside of the pool wall, with the liner sandwiched between gasket and wall. To align these skimmer parts with the pool's precut skimmer hole, push two screws through the faceplate, gasket, liner and wall, and into the skimmer housing outside the pool. Tighten the two screws, then add the remaining screws, but avoid overtightening, which could crack the faceplate. When the skimmer is firmly attached, use a utility knife to cut away the liner inside the faceplate opening.

At the precut hole for the return fitting, cut away a piece of the liner slightly smaller than the hole. Insert the dome-shaped inner portion of the return assembly (inset) through the hole, and thread the outer portion onto it, tightening it firmly with channel-joint pliers or an adjustable wrench.

Connect the skimmer and the return assemblies to the filter pump with screw-on hoses.

Hot Tubs: A Bit of Rome at Home

Bathing as a social event is scarcely a new idea. Second Century Roman men played chess, gossiped and arranged affairs of state in the famous baths of Caracella, whose 66 marble-walled rooms accommodated 3,000 bathers. And modern Japanese men, women and children follow the age-old custom of bathing communally, in 20,000 or so public bath houses.

The hot tub simply perpetuates this ancient tradition, albeit on a more modest scale. When placed outdoors its installation is relatively simple. Its parts consist of a wooden tub, which you can purchase as a kit or build yourself, and a plumbing support system whose components—water pump, filter, heater—are like those used for a swimming pool.

Choose the hot-tub site with care, taking into account privacy and convenience to the house as well as several practical factors. The tub and its support system must be less than 20 feet apart and accessible to utility lines. For safety, however, do not place the tub directly over or under these lines. Also consider the tub's exposure to sun and wind.

The tremendous weight of a filled tub makes a stable foundation essential. Consult the local building inspector about code stipulations, building permits and the best foundation for your soil (see page 104 for two typical foundations).

You can purchase a prefabricated hot-tub kit that has all the wooden parts cut and shaped to size and includes its own plumbing, or you can cut the parts yourself. The popularity of hot tubs has made kits plentiful, but not all are milled well, so if you decide to buy a kit, check with the local Better Business Bureau for any reports on the manufacturer. It is a good idea, too, to ask the manufacturer for the names of local people who have used the kit, and if possible to see their tubs.

If you wish to mill the wooden parts yourself, use kiln-dried redwood, cypress, cedar, teak or oak. You will need 2-by-8s, 2-by-10s or 2-by-12s for the flooring, and 2-by-10s for the seats, 2-by-6s for the vertical slats (staves), and redwood or pressure-treated 4-by-4s for the joists on which the floor rests. You will also need ⅜-inch dowels for the pegs that fasten the floorboards together, in lieu of nails or glue. And to hold the staves together,

you will need hoops of solid-core steel rod, ½ inch in diameter, with threaded ends that fit into tightening lugs. (For tubs more than 6 feet in diameter, you will need double hoops and lugs.)

The likeliest source for this hardware is a foundry or a maker of wooden barrels or water tanks. You will have to specify the diameter of your tub so the hoops can be cut to length and curved to fit it.

Because the wooden parts of the tub must be beveled, grooved and planed to fit together into a circular shape, and because the tub's watertight seal depends largely on the swelling of the wet wood, the shaping of the wood parts must be precise. Use stationary power tools—a table saw or jointer—if you cut the parts at home. Otherwise, have them cut to your specifications at a lumber mill.

For the support system, select components that were designed to work together. Many hot-tub manufacturers will sell their support systems separately, complete with instructions for installation. Choose a system appropriate to the size of your tub, the number of jets desired, the probable frequency of use, the climate of your area and the cheapest local source of energy.

The system shown opposite is a simple one, but you can add special features—for example, an air blower for increased jet action. Holes for connecting this equipment to the tub should be drilled in the staves before the tub is assembled. Although shown here uncovered, the support system should in fact be housed in a ventilated boxlike cover, to camouflage and protect it.

When the tub is finished, use a garden sprinkler to fill it; the sprinkler will moisten the walls gradually, so the staves will expand and tighten evenly. (In redwood tubs, the wood's red "bleeding" can continue up to a year before the water is clear; scrubbing the surface may speed the process.) The tub will probably leak for three days to two weeks, until its parts have swelled completely. If leaking persists, check to make sure the staves are evenly spaced and firmly seated against the floor, and that the foundation has not settled. Tightening the bottom hoop or adding another hoop just below or above it will often stop leaks.

Cleaning a Hot Tub and Protecting Its Parts

For years of trouble-free enjoyment, hot tubs need proper care. In general, they are maintained much as swimming pools are (pages 115-117). Manufacturers of support systems generally provide instructions for cleaning filters and adjusting water levels, as well as a water-testing kit for monitoring the water chemistry. Monitoring is essential and should be done daily because the high temperature of the water in a hot tub makes it an ideal breeding ground for algae and bacteria. In addition, the tub should be drained every three to six months, depending on the frequency of use, and scrubbed down with baking soda and a stiff brush to remove the thin film that will accumulate despite the best daily maintenance.

If keeping the tub clean is of primary importance, protecting it from damage by inclement weather runs a close second. In a very cold climate, that means winterizing both the tub and its support system.

If you intend to continue using the hot tub through the cold months, insulate all of the plumbing lines with thermostatically controlled electric insulation tape, which is available at building-supply stores. If possible, install the support system indoors; otherwise, house it and insulate it with a blanket of polystyrene foam ½ inch to 2 inches thick.

If you do not plan to use the tub through the winter, drain the support system completely but leave 2 inches of water in the bottom of the tub, to prevent the critical bottom joints from shrinking. Also wrap the tub in a heavy canvas blanket.

No matter where you live, in whatever climate, keep the exterior of the tub in good condition by rubbing it with generous amounts of linseed oil two or three times a year.

Anatomy of a hot-tub system. In this free-standing wooden hot tub, 2-by-8 floorboards form a circle 1½ inches smaller than the tub's overall diameter. The boards are edge-joined at the center, and also 2 inches from each end, with ⅜-inch dowels, each 3 inches long, driven into holes drilled 1½ inches deep. Before assembly, the curved edges are planed on the underside starting 2 inches from the edge, to taper them to a thickness of 1⁷⁄₁₆ inches.

Vertical 2-by-6 boards for staves are dadoed (grooved) 3 inches up from the bottom, to accept the tapered edge of the floor (*inset*); the dadoes are cut ¾ inch deep and 1⁷⁄₁₆ inches wide. The long edges of each stave are beveled

inward slightly; to calculate the angle of this bevel, divide the tub circumference in inches by the width of a stave, round the result up to the nearest whole number, and divide this number into 180°. Steel hoops with tightening lugs are spaced about a foot apart, to squeeze the entire structure together.

The tub rests on—but is not nailed to—4-by-4 redwood or pressure-treated joists that transfer the tub's weight directly to the foundation. These joists also let air circulate beneath the staves and floorboards, discouraging rot. A 6-foot tub needs three joists; for tubs 6 to 10 feet in diameter, use four joists. The bench-type seats are cut from 2-by-10 boards, curved to fit

the tub, and are supported by vertical legs. For easy access, lean a ladder against the side of the tub or build a deck around it (*pages 107-111*).

In this typical support system, the water flows through a 1½-inch pipe to a leaf trap, then into the pump, which forces it through a filter, into the heater, and back to the tub via jets. The system is drained through a hose attached to the gate or three-way valve; the water above the outlet hole is pumped out and the rest is diluted and flushed out a second and sometimes even a third time. (In areas that suffer from water shortages, where this lavish use of water is not permitted, hot tubs are drained simply by the removal of a plug in the bottom of the tub.)

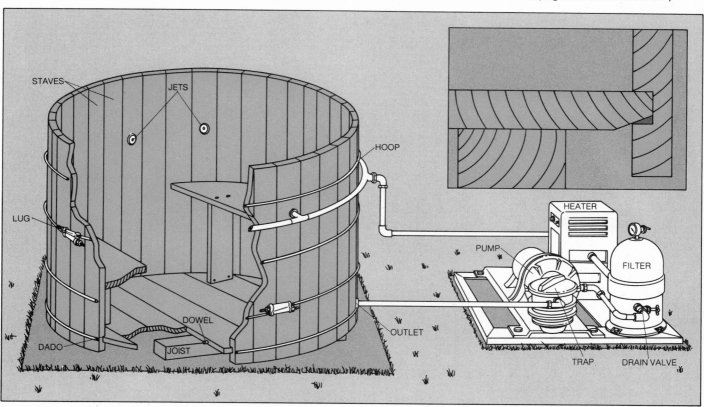

Safety Rules of Vital Importance

Though nothing may seem more soothing for sore muscles or after a stressful day, hot tubs in fact can be hazardous to your health, and should be used with care. Several fatalities have prompted doctors to remind hot-tub owners that immersion in water of over 100° for long periods can be dangerous, especially for persons with heart ailments.

As body temperature rises, veins at the surface of the skin dilate, causing less blood to return to the heart. As a result, the supply of oxygen-carrying blood reaching the brain is reduced and a dangerous drowsiness sets in that could lead to shock. This sequence of events happens most speedily when the body is already overheated—after jogging, for instance, or tennis.

In addition to those with heart or circulatory problems, diabetics, pregnant women and anyone overweight should consult a doctor before using a hot tub.

Never let your tub's water temperature rise above 104°—most doctors recommend 100° to 101° for adults, 98° for children under five. Never drink alcoholic beverages in the tub, and always take a cool shower after using the tub to lower body temperature to normal.

Matching the Foundation to the Soil

A foundation for dense clay soil. If your soil contains a heavy concentration of clay, this crushed-stone foundation provides adequate support for a hot tub. A square bed approximately 10 inches deep is filled with the stone. A drainage pipe at the base of the bed—usually of 4-inch perforated plastic—carries away standing water. The pipe extends out from the bed in a slightly downhill trench and is positioned so that the tub's weight does not rest on it.

Before installing the tub, tamp the crushed stone thoroughly to prevent later settling, and to make sure that the surface is level.

A foundation for loose soil. If your soil is sandy or loamy, this 10-inch-deep concrete foundation bed is ideal. It consists of 6 inches of gravel, covered by a layer of reinforcing wire mesh topped by a 4-inch-thick pad of concrete. The concrete surface slopes slightly for drainage.

Caution: In an area that has very cold winters, the foundation may have to be deeper to prevent cracking. Consult a local building inspector.

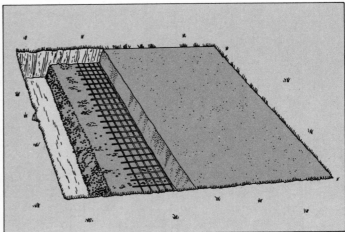

The Art of Making a Watertight Tub

1 **Fitting the floorboards together.** Level the joists and rest the floorboards on them, placing the boards at right angles to the joists, in order and with their planed edges down. Insert dowels in the predrilled holes along the board edges and tap the boards together with a rubber mallet, leaving a gap of about $1/16$ inch between them to allow for later swelling; use tongue depressors or wood shingles as temporary shims. When the circular floor is assembled, nail two temporary 1-inch-thick braces across it to secure the boards; do not drive the nails completely through the floor. (The dowels are not glued in.)

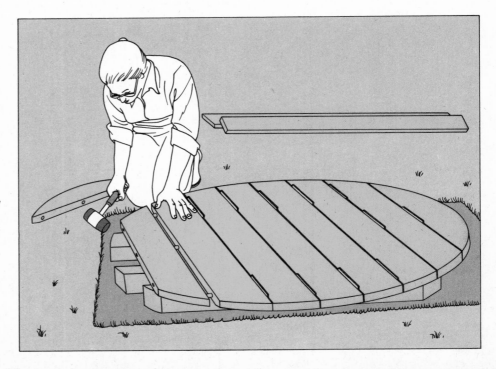

2 Marking placement guides. As an aid to setting staves against the floor, use a pencil and combination square to scribe a line around the floor—usually about ¾ inch in from the edge. Mark on this line the approximate position of any staves that have predrilled holes for the plumbing system. Check to make sure joists and floorboards run perpendicular to each other and that joists are short enough to clear the edge of the floor at both ends by about 1½ inches so they will not interfere with the staves.

If you have milled your own staves, drill holes in them, following the specifications provided by the manufacturer of the support system for size and location. Center each hole on a stave and make sure you do not angle the bit as you drill.

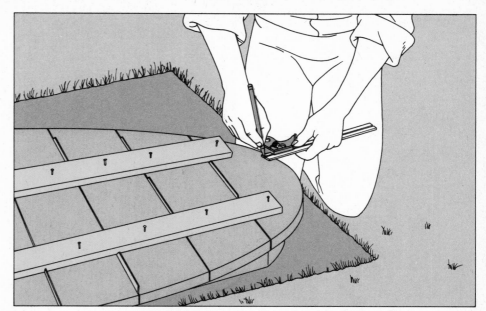

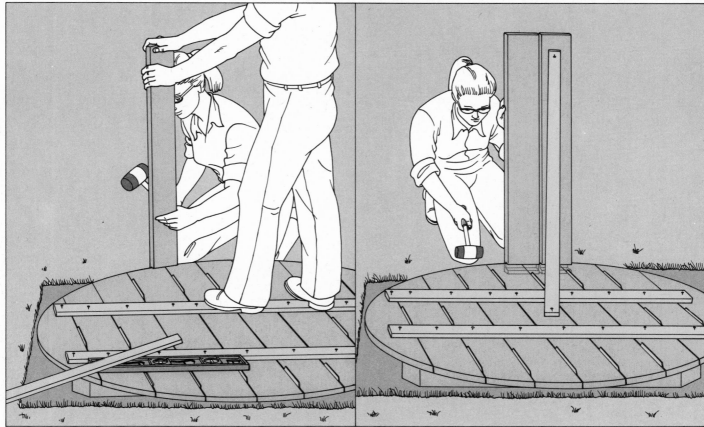

3 Setting the staves. Squeeze a bead of roofing mastic along the lower edge of the dado on a single stave, and slide the stave onto the edge of the floor, directly over the joint between two floorboards. Have a helper hold the stave steady while you gently tap it about halfway onto the floorboard with a rubber mallet *(left)*; use the scribed guideline on the floor to gauge this dis-

tance. Brace the stave upright, perpendicular to the floor, by angling a 1-by-2 between the stave and floor; use fourpenny nails driven into both ends of the brace to hold it in place, but be very careful not to drive the nails all the way through the stave or floor. Continue setting the remaining staves in the same way, bracing where it is necessary to ensure that they remain

plumb. As each stave is added, tap it lightly just below the dado to move it toward the adjacent stave, so that the bottoms of the staves are as close together as possible *(right)*. Keep the upper ends of the staves from leaning outward by pulling them together with a cord tied around fourpenny nails that have been driven part of the way through the tops of the staves.

4 **Fitting the last stave.** When all staves but one are in place, measure the outside width of the remaining gap, and set a T bevel against each of the two staves framing the gap to determine the exact angles of the bevel on each side. Trim the last stave precisely to this size with a table saw, or have a mill do the job. Tap the trimmed stave into place as in Step 3, page 105.

5 **Positioning the hoops.** At four points evenly spaced around the outside of the tub, about ½ inch below the center of the dado, drive eight-penny nails partway through the staves. Thread the ends of a hoop into a lug, rest the hoop on the nails and position the lug so that it spans two staves. Tighten the nuts on either side of the lug alternately and evenly until the hoop fits against the staves. Use the same technique to install the remaining hoops, spacing them about a foot apart and staggering the positions of the lugs around the tub. When all the hoops are in place, remove all the shims, braces, cords and nails from the structure. Align all the staves by tapping them gently in or out until the inside surface of the tub is smooth.

6 **Rounding and finishing the tub.** With a rubber mallet, set each stave firmly against the floor by hammering the staves at the dado line, striking the bottom hoop to cushion and distribute the force of the blows. From the point where you begin, work a quarter of the way around the tub in both directions. Then change your position and, from the opposite side of the tub, set the remaining staves on the tub's other half in the same fashion. Have a helper tighten the hoop as you work, to fit the tub's new dimensions. When the bottoms of the staves are in place, work your way up the sides of the tub, setting staves at each successive hoop but gradually putting less pressure on both the staves and the hoops as you near the top.

Smooth the rim of the tub by hand—first with a rasp and then with fine-grit sandpaper. Clean out any debris from inside the tub and saturate its outside with boiled linseed oil.

A Wood Deck for Hot Tub or Pool

A wooden deck designed for your house and land can turn a sloping site into a level surface for various outdoor activities, while providing convenient access to a pool or hot tub.

For a deck that will remain strong and attractive for many years, use good grades of wood: Structural No. 1 for beams and joists, Select Structural planks for the deck. Choose wood that is resistant to decay, warp and wear, such as Douglas fir, redwood or western red cedar. For below-ground posts—and preferably for the above-ground structure too —use pressure-treated wood. For added protection where the end grain of lumber will be exposed or in the ground, especially where fresh cuts have been made, soak the ends with wood preservative. Use hardware made of galvanized steel or other corrosion-resistant metal.

A deck attached to a house is usually considered an addition to the house, so it will probably have to meet building-code requirements and you will need a building permit. The deck shown here is designed to support a live load—the weight of people, furniture, snow and other nonstructural elements—of 60 pounds per square foot. This will conform to most local codes but check with your authorities before drawing the plans to accompany your permit application.

Before building the deck, you must remove existing stairs to the house. Then lay out the positions of the supporting posts, using stakes and string to get the corners exactly square *(page 29)*. Set the posts in holes 16 inches square and at least 3 feet deep, using the technique described on pages 50-51 but substituting 8 inches of concrete for the gravel and flat rock. In cold regions, deeper holes may be needed so the bottoms of posts reach below the frost line. The maximum distance between posts is 8 feet.

The beams are a double layer of the same lumber used for the joists, nailed together with 16-penny nails along each edge, 1½ inches in from the edge and 12 inches apart. Bend over the nail points that protrude through the beam. Consult the table *(right)* to determine the size, span and spacing of the joists.

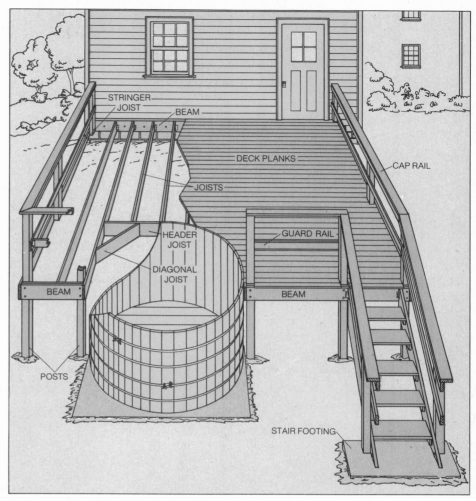

Anatomy of a deck. This hillside deck, which links a hot tub with a house, rests on a beam bolted to the house and on beams bolted to 4-by-4 posts set in concrete and soil. The beams—here, double 2-by-8s—support 2-by-8 joists attached to the beams with steel framing connectors. A header joist and two diagonals frame the tub bay.

The 2-by-4 deck planks are nailed across the joists with narrow spaces between them for drainage. The stairs to the ground rest on 2-by-8 stringers attached to the beam at the top with steel framing connectors and secured at the bottom to steel framing anchors set in a concrete footing. The stair treads are nailed to wooden cleats that have been nailed to the stringers. The guardrails are 2-by-4s nailed to the deck posts and to two other 4-by-4 posts bolted to the bottom of the stairs. A 2-by-6 cap rail tops off the railing and protects the ends of the posts.

Joist Specifications

Joist size	Maximum spans by size and spacing Joist spacing, center to center	Maximum joist span
2 × 6	16″	8′6″
2 × 6	24″	6′10″
2 × 8	16″	11′3″
2 × 8	24″	9′2″
2 × 10	16″	14′3″
2 × 10	24″	11′8″

Framing to Support a Deck

1 Attaching a beam to the house. Cut the beam for the house side of the deck to the desired length and drill ½-inch boltholes near its center line at 12-inch intervals. Use wood scraps to prop the beam against the house wall 1½ inches below the desired height of the finished deck. Mark through the boltholes and remove the beam. If the house wall at this level is wood, drill ⅜-inch pilot holes in the wall and attach the beam with ½-inch lag bolts, 6 inches long.

If the house wall is cinder block (*inset, top*), use a ½-inch star drill to cut holes all the way through the wall. For each hole make a back-up block 8 inches long from 2-by-8 lumber, drilling a ½-inch hole centered in each block. Anchor the beam to the wall with 14-inch lengths of ½-inch threaded rod, using nuts and washers on each end. If the house wall at this level is brick or poured concrete (*inset, bottom*), drill ¾-inch holes with a masonry bit or star drill. Using lead expansion shields, fasten the beam to the wall with ½-inch lag bolts, 6 inches long.

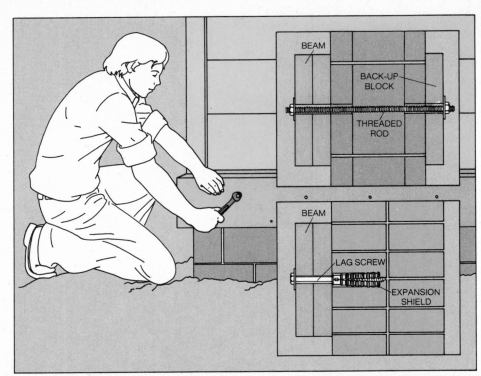

2 Attaching beams to posts. Position the beams for the front edge of the deck against their supporting posts, set in concrete and soil. Anchor each beam temporarily with nails and drill ½-inch holes through the beam and post with an auger bit. Fasten the beam to each post with two ½-inch carriage bolts, 6 inches long. Similarly attach a stringer joist to the outside of each corner post, using a steel framing connector (*inset*) to attach the other end to the beam on the house.

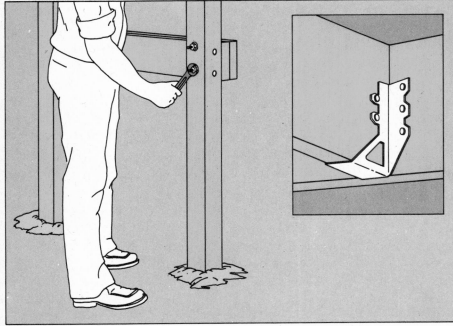

Mark where joists will meet the beams at the front and back; nail framing connectors to the beams at these points. Lift the joists into the connectors and nail them in place.

To make a bay for a hot tub or above-ground pool, use framing connectors to hang a header joist between the joists at each side of the bay. If the width of the bay exceeds 4 feet, use a doubled header joist. Hang regular joists between this joist and the rear beam.

3 Nailing diagonal joists. To support a curved section of deck around a hot tub or pool, nail diagonal joists across the right angles formed by the regular joists and the short header joist. Cut the ends of the diagonal joists at a 45° angle. Secure each end to the deck framing with three 16-penny nails.

Bolt a 4-by-4 railing-support post to the inside of each stringer joist where it meets the beam on the house, and bolt additional posts to the insides of stringers or beams so the maximum interval between railing supports is 4 feet. Use two ½-inch carriage bolts, 6 inches long, to secure each post to the frame, and trim all posts to a height of 36 inches above the top of the frame.

CLEAT

SPACER

How to Install the Decking

1 Nailing the decking. Starting against the house wall, nail decking across the joists with 12-penny galvanized-steel or aluminum nails, using two nails at each joist. Space the deck boards ³⁄₁₆ inch apart for drainage by temporarily putting scraps of ³⁄₁₆-inch hardboard between them. At the edge of the deck, allow the boards to overlap the stringer joists an inch or more. When all the decking is laid, mark a straight line across each side of the deck and saw off all the irregular ends in a single cut. If you must use more than one board to span the deck, join the boards over a joist and stagger the joists so they do not fall in a single line across one joist. Do not attach the last plank at the deck edge until after you install stair stringers *(page 110).*

Before laying the decking around a post *(inset),* nail a short 2-by-2 cleat to the post to support the decking; the grain of the cleat should run horizontally. Drill two ⅛-inch holes through each cleat to keep it from splitting when it is nailed, and use two 12-penny nails to secure it.

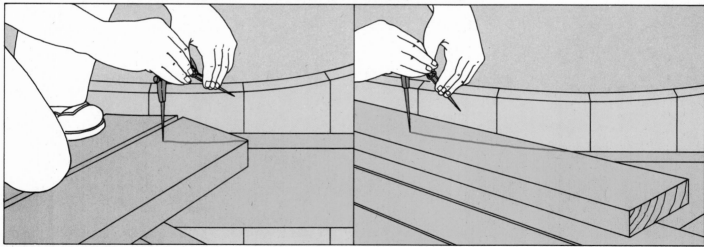

2 Cutting irregular ends. When decking meets a rounded object, such as a hot tub, use a scriber to transfer the curve to the deck board before nailing it down. Make the cut with a saber saw.

If the curve falls across the end of a board *(above, left),* position the board alongside the last nailed board, with the correct space between them and with one corner of the board against the tub wall. Hold the scriber parallel with the long

edge of the board, one point against the tub wall, the other on the board. Move the scriber along the wall to transfer the curve to the board. Be sure the board will still cover the necessary distance on the deck after the end is cut off along the marked curve.

When the curve falls along the edge of a board *(above, right),* position it for scribing by placing it on top of the last nailed board and sliding it

toward the tub until the tub and the board meet; be certain the overlapping boards remain parallel. Measure the width of the lip between the two boards and set the scriber ¼ inch wider than this distance. Place one point of the scriber against the tub wall and the other on the board to be cut. Holding the scriber so that it is always perpendicular to the overlapping boards, move it along the tub wall, transferring the curve of the tub wall to the board to be cut.

A Stairway to the Deck

1 **Making a footing for the stairs.** To anchor the bottom of the stairs to the ground, embed steel framing anchors in a concrete footing, positioning the anchors so their distance from the deck is at least equal to the deck height. (A longer stairway with wide treads and short risers is safer when the steps are wet.)

For the footing, dig a hole that reaches below the frost line, and position it so the framing anchors will fall about 1 foot in from its back edge. Make the footing about 1 foot wider than the overall width of the stairs, and 3 or 4 feet from front to back. Raise it above the ground 1½ inches by framing the top temporarily with 1-by-2s fastened to corner stakes, leveling the top of this frame with a carpenter's level. Fill the hole with cement and embed framing anchors in it, setting the top wings 1½ inches apart to accommodate the thickness of the stair stringers.

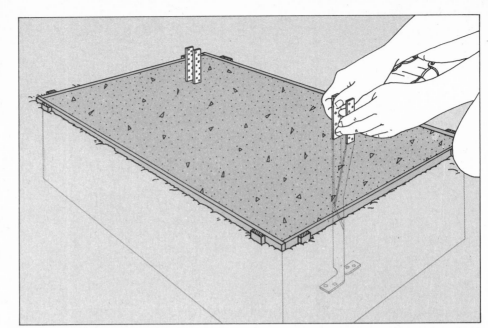

2 **Marking the stringers.** Rest one end of a 2-by-8, turned on edge, against the edge of the deck beam; rest a corner of the opposite end on the concrete footing about 4 inches beyond a framing anchor and lined up with the anchor wings. Hold a level vertical at the top end of the board, flush with the deck beam, and draw a diagonal line to mark the cut at the top of the stringer.

With the board still in position, mark the bottom of the stringer by holding the level vertical at the point where the corner rests on the concrete footing. Draw a vertical line up across the stringer and, at the point where that line intersects the top edge, draw a second (horizontal) line at right angles to the first (inset). Use this second line to cut the bottom of the stringer.

Mark and cut a second stringer, identical to the first. Join the stringers to the deck beam with steel framing connectors and to the wings of the framing anchors with nails.

3 **Attaching cleats for stair treads.** Using 10-penny nails, fasten 2-by-3 cleats, each about 8 inches long, to both stringers. To calculate the number of cleats needed on each stringer, measure the vertical distance, in inches, from the concrete footing to the top of the deck; use a level plank extending out from the deck as a point of reference. Divide this vertical distance by the height you have selected for the risers—about 8 inches if the stairs rise at 45°, as shown. Round off the result to the nearest whole number. This is the number of intervals between steps; subtract 1 to find the number of stair treads you need, and the number of pairs of cleats.

To calculate the exact interval between cleats, divide the number of intervals into the vertical distance from the footing to the top of the deck. Mark these intervals on the stringers and position the cleats 1½ inches below them, to allow for the thickness of the stair tread.

When the cleats are nailed in place, cut 2-by-10 treads to fit between them and nail the treads to the cleats, positioned flush with the top edges of the stringers. To support stair rails, bolt a 4-by-4 post to the bottom of each stringer, flush with the corner where the lower edge of the stringer meets the footing.

Building Guardrails for Added Safety

Completing the rail assemblies. Using a crosscut saw, cut the rail posts around the deck to a uniform height and miter the stair-rail posts at the same angle as the stringers. Nail two 2-by-4 guardrails to the insides of the stair-way posts, one guardrail at the midpoint, the other flush with the tops of the posts. Nail a 2-by-6 cap rail to the top guardrail.

Nail similar guardrails and cap rails around the edge of the deck. If a guardrail requires more than one piece of lumber, cut so that the joints fall at the posts; for cap rails, locate the joints between posts so that the end grain of the posts will be protected from rain.

The Best of Care for an Above- or In-ground Pool

The adage, "An ounce of prevention is worth a pound of cure," applies especially to maintaining a home swimming pool. Without attention, the inside of the pool will become dirt- and algae-covered, the filtration system clogged, the water corrosive. Correcting this condition is time-consuming and expensive, but the problem can be avoided with a few routine chores that keep the pool and its water safe, clean and inviting.

The maintenance routine is the same for all three types of swimming pools—above-, on- or in-ground. Above-ground pools (page 96) consist of a vinyl liner held by a wall of fiberglass or metal. On-ground pools are similar in construction but are sunk into the ground at one end, to form a deep area. Some in-ground pools are constructed in the same manner as on-ground pools but sunk completely below grade. More often, however, they consist of a concrete bowl cast in an excavation. Hot tubs and home spas require much the same care as pools.

One of the basic maintenance chores is to keep the sides and bottom of the pool free of the dirt that settles from the air or enters on swimmers' bodies. While most of this material is filtered out, some clings to the pool interior. This dirt is most easily removed by a weekly brushing of the pool and a weekly vacuuming with a special hose, vacuum head and pole connected to the filter system. In addition, the sides of the pool at the water line are apt to be soiled by a ring of suntan lotion or other oil that floats on the water. Cleaning this ring too is a once-a-week chore, requiring a sponge and a cleaner sold at pool-supply stores.

Many pools are equipped with automatic cleaning devices that take care of one or both of these problems, the dirt and the oil. Some of the devices are small robots; one kind scuttles along the bottom and up the pool sides. Other robots float on the water with hoses dangling below; water surges through the hoses to propel them around to scour the walls. A third device directs jets of water from underwater outlets against the sides and bottom of the pool. Each works differently and should be used and cared for according to the maker's instructions.

In addition to being routinely cleaned, pools should also be routinely inspected for flaws in their surfaces. Small tears in a vinyl liner and cracks in the plaster lining of a concrete pool should be promptly repaired to prevent further damage. Vinyl liners require a repair kit, consisting of patches and an underwater adhesive for applying them. To repair the plaster lining of a concrete pool, you can buy a premixed underwater plaster at pool-supply stores. Or you can mix it yourself, using 1 part white cement and 2 parts white marble dust, and adding enough mason's antihydro liquid to make a doughlike consistency. But eventually the surface of any pool will need replacement. A new vinyl liner will have to be installed, or old plaster will have to be sandblasted off and a new coat applied.

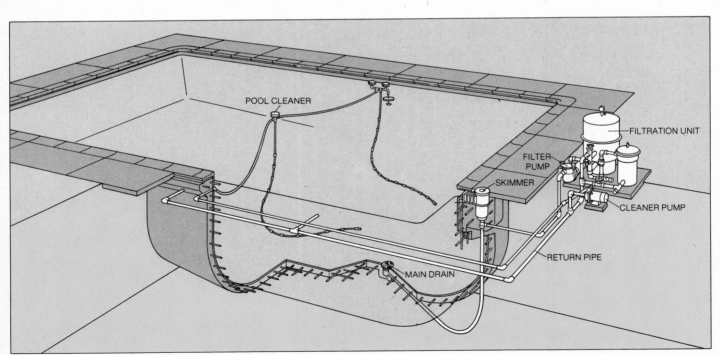

Anatomy of an in-ground pool. In this typical reinforced-concrete swimming pool, outlets and accessories for the maintenance of the pool are built into its design. Pipes from a main drain in the bottom of the pool and from a skimmer at the water's edge carry water to a filter pump, which forces the water through a filtration unit and sends it back to the pool through a return pipe. A branch on the return pipe also sends water to a second pump, where it is forced, under pressure, into an automatic pool cleaner that floats on the surface of the water. The deck is highest right around the pool and then slopes away, to prevent dirty water at the edges of the pool from running into the pool.

Keeping the Pool Clean

1 Emptying the skimmer basket. Once a week or oftener, lift off the cover of the skimmer, remove the basket and wipe out any accumulated debris. Some baskets have a floating collar, called a weir, that keeps debris from floating back out into the pool; remove the weir before emptying the basket. Brush the walls and bottom of the pool next, with a pole-mounted pool brush.

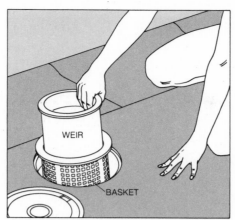

2 Assembling the vacuum. Set the flow control of the skimmer to skim, replace the basket without the weir and fit the vacuum plate inside the skimmer (*inset*). With the filtration system running, attach the vacuum hose to the vacuum head and submerge the assembly, on its pole, in the water. Feed the rest of the hose into the water and allow the hose to fill completely. Then hold your hand over the end of the hose, draw it out of the water, submerge it again in the water-filled skimmer and fit the hose to the vacuum plate. Note: The flow controls on skimmers vary from model to model—ask the installer or manufacturer to instruct you on the operation of yours.

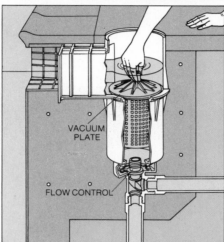

Safety Rules for Pools

☐ All nonswimmers in the family should learn to swim as soon as possible, and in the meantime use life jackets, not inflatable toys, for support.
☐ Do not permit children to enter the pool unless a swimmer is present, and keep an eye on them at all times.
☐ Do not swim alone or during electrical storms.
☐ Keep first-aid supplies handy. Family members who are old enough should learn artificial respiration and cardio-pulmonary resuscitation.
☐ Keep a ring buoy and a shepherd's-hook lifesaving pole near the pool.
☐ Keep clutter such as hoses and toys away from the edge of the pool.
☐ Replace the cover of the skimmer immediately after you have cleaned it.
☐ Keep all glass, sharp objects and plug-in electrical equipment far away from the pool.
☐ Fence the pool to prevent unauthorized access; check local codes regarding fence heights and gate locks.
☐ Use common sense when diving. Dive only at the deep end; dive only from the front end of a diving board and only after swimmers are clear.
☐ Do not substitute a larger or springier board for the one provided with the pool—most are matched to the particular pool's shape and depth.
☐ Get a professional to change the bulb in an underwater pool light.

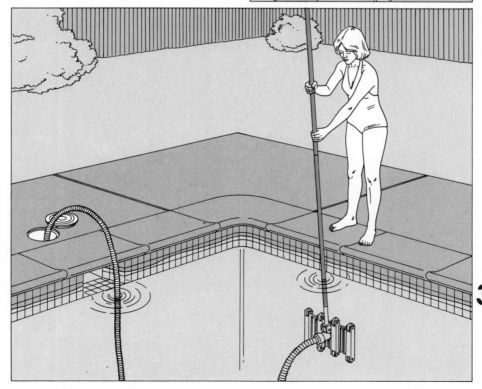

3 Vacuuming the pool. With the pool pole, guide the vacuum down the side of the pool and over to the center; then draw it toward you along the bottom and up the side. Stop just below the surface of the water and make a second stroke parallel to the first, down the side and across the bottom to the middle of the pool. Proceed in this fashion all around the pool perimeter.

Patching a Pool Lined with Plaster

Using underwater pool plaster. Push a fistful of underwater pool plaster into the crack or hole in the plaster coating and smooth it with a trowel. Give the mixture 24 hours to set before touching it. To paint over the patch, drain the pool until the water line is below the repair.

Repairing a Torn Vinyl Liner

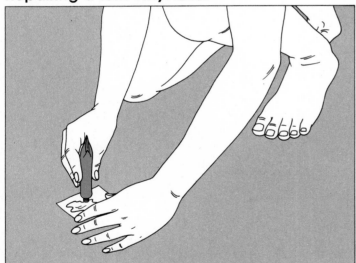

1 **Applying glue to a patch.** Cut a vinyl patch to extend 1 inch beyond any part of a rip or tear in the side or bottom of a vinyl-lined pool. Wipe the damaged area with a clean cloth. Spread vinyl adhesive in a thin layer onto the patch.

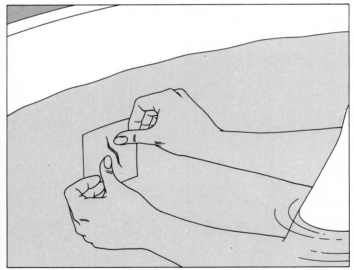

2 **Applying the patch.** Place the patch over the damaged area, underwater, and rub it from the middle outward to the edges to squeeze water from between the patch and the pool liner.

To make a large patch easier to handle, fold it in half—adhesive side in—before submerging it in the pool. Then unfold it and place it over the rip or tear. For tears longer than 1 foot, hire pool-service professionals; they will use a machine that heat-seals the vinyl in place.

Keeping Water Chemically Pure

To be suitable for swimming, water must be more than just comfortably wet. It must act as a disinfectant to kill any bacteria that enter the water and it should present an inhospitable environment to algae. It should be able to neutralize chemical contaminants while itself remaining chemically neutral, so as not to corrode pipes and pool interiors. And it must do all these things without irritating human eyes or other parts of the body.

Swimming-pool water is treated with chemicals to give it all these attributes. Some chemicals are used frequently and their levels can be monitored with a simple poolside test kit *(page 116)*. Others require elaborate tests that can be performed only by pool-service experts.

The principal chemical used is chlorine, a powerful disinfectant that oxidizes—in effect, burns—bacteria, algae and a wide range of chemical contaminants. It is the same sanitizing chemical used in most city water systems. Chlorine itself is a deadly green gas, but for residential use it is combined with other chemicals that turn it into a safe and easily handled liquid or solid.

Unfortunately, in the process of disinfecting the water, chlorine changes form and either disappears from the water entirely or remains in the water but loses its disinfecting properties. Sunlight drives it from the water, and nitrogen—usually in the form of ammonia from perspiration or urine—neutralizes it. To counter the effect of sun on the chlorine level, a stabilizer—cyanuric acid—is added to the water, shielding the chlorine from the sun's ultraviolet rays; but new chlorine must constantly be added to the water to replace that lost to contaminants or neutralized by nitrogen. The proper balance is most easily maintained with chlorine-impregnated tablets or sticks that dissolve slowly in the skimmer basket or in a floating dispenser.

Even the chlorine that is neutralized by nitrogen eventually reaches unacceptable levels and must be removed. It is this neutralized chlorine that produces the unwanted effects that are usually blamed on overchlorination—the strong chlorine odor and the burning, reddened eyes. Paradoxically, to remove the excessive chlorine more chlorine is added, quickly and in large doses that boost the chlorine level to five times normal. This process, called superchlorination, breaks up the chlorine-nitrogen combination; some of the freed chlorine is then drawn off by the sun, returning the pool's chlorine level to normal. Superchlorination takes place overnight, during which time the pool should not be used.

A second chemical property that must be maintained in pool water is the balance between acidity and alkalinity, commonly referred to as the pH level. Ideally, swimming-pool water should be slightly alkaline, to prevent it from eating into metal fittings, ladders, pipes, tanks and pumps and the pool walls and bottom. But it should not be so alkaline as to interfere with the action of the chlorine.

The pH balance is maintained by the addition of acid or alkaline substances to the water to correct an imbalance, as indicated by tests. But the stability of the balance will be affected by what is called the water's total alkalinity, the actual measure—in parts per million (ppm)—of its natural alkaline content. If the total alkalinity reading is too low, the introduction of even small amounts of alkaline or acid material into the pool—from swimmers' bodies, for example—will be enough to tip the pH level off balance. The pH level resists change better when the total alkalinity reading is correct.

The third chemical characteristic of the water that must be controlled is its hardness, that is, the amount of dissolved minerals it contains. Chief among these is calcium, which must be kept at a level that will complement the water's total alkalinity. Other minerals such as iron, manganese and copper normally do not present problems, but if their levels are too high they can cause staining and will require chemical treatments.

While chlorine usually kills algae spores, occasionally these spores will grow inside minute air bubbles on the sides of the pool. To break up these bubbles and prevent algae growth, a wetting agent is added to the water.

The treatment of water in hot tubs and home spas is virtually the same as for swimming-pool water. The amounts of chemicals are reduced proportionately and the wetting agent is not used.

Safety with Pool Chemicals

Working with any chemicals can be hazardous, but pool maintenance is especially tricky because several of the chemicals are not compatible and must not be mixed together before being added to the water. Used individually, they are safe if normal caution is exercised, but if mixed they can explode or exude deadly gas. Take time to read the label instructions and precautions carefully. Other safety rules to observe include:

☐ When adding several chemicals to the pool, allow at least an hour between treatments.

☐ Store pool chemicals in a dry place out of the reach of children.

☐ Do not leave combustible materials —a paper cup, for example—inside a container holding a pool chemical.

☐ Avoid touching any of the chemicals or inhaling their fumes or dust, and wash your hands after use.

Using a test kit. A complete poolside test kit has two vials—one for testing the amount of chlorine in the water and the second for testing the pH balance. Pool water is placed in the vials, and tablets or drops of test solutions are added to the samples. The water changes color and the color is compared to color samples provided alongside the vials.

A number corresponding to the color that most closely resembles the color of the water indicates the amount of chlorine or the relative pH balance. For chlorine, the number indicates parts per million (ppm) by weight; in other words, how many pounds of chlorine would be found in a million pounds of the sample water. The pH balance—acidity or alkalinity—is indicated on a scale from 0 to 14, on which 0 is very acid, 14 is very alkaline and 7 is neutral.

Since chlorine affects the pH test chemicals, the chlorine level should be determined first; the water sample for the pH test is then dosed with a solution that compensates for the chlorine.

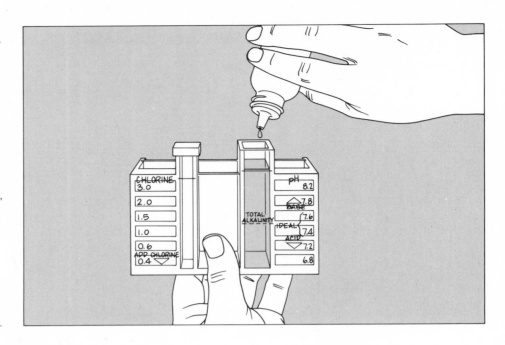

Tests that Reveal Chemical Imbalance

| Measurement | Ideal | Too High | | Too Low | |
		Problem	Treatment	Problem	Treatment
Chlorine	1 to 1.5 ppm	No danger, but wastes chlorine	Discontinue chlorination until the reading drops to 1.5 ppm; reinstitute continuous chlorination at a lower rate by using fewer sticks or tablets	Unhygienic	Increase rate of chlorination by using more sticks or tablets
pH balance	7.4 to 7.6 for plaster-lined pools; 7.4 for vinyl-lined pools	Affects chlorine efficiency; mineral deposits form on pool and parts	Add pH reducer	Irritates eyes; corrodes pool and its parts	Add pH increaser
Total alkalinity	80 to 125 ppm for plaster; 125 to 150 ppm for vinyl	Mineral deposits form on pool and parts	Add alkalinity reducer, wait an hour; add pH increaser	pH balance is prone to shift excessively	Add alkalinity increaser
Stabilizer level	40 to 60 ppm	Chlorine is less efficient above 100 ppm	Dilute by removing some pool water and replacing with fresh water	Chlorine dissipates	Add stabilizer
Calcium hardness	200 to 275 ppm for plaster; 175 to 225 for vinyl	Mineral deposits form on pool and parts	Dilute by removing some pool water and replacing with fresh water	Corrodes pool and its parts	Add calcium

A reference chart for balanced water. Listed vertically are the five chemical levels that are routinely measured to test the condition of pool water. Read across the table to find their ideal levels as well as the potential problems and the appropriate corrective treatment. The first three measurements should be taken every two days at poolside. When corrective treatment is in progress or unusual conditions exist, such as more bathers than normal or recent heavy rains, take readings more often. Hot tubs also need more frequent testing. At the start of each swimming season and toward the end, take a sample of pool water to a pool-service store for analysis of all five measurements to spot deficiencies before they cause difficulty. Unusual problems should also be tested professionally. Such tests are usually done without charge.

A Choice of Chemicals to Improve the Water

Chemical	Description and purpose	Amount per 1000 gallons	Application
Trichloro-s-triazenetrione, also called trichlor, tri-chloroisocyanurate, TCC, TCCA; sticks or tablets	Chlorine for continuous chlorination; also contains stabilizer	Sticks, 1 ounce; tablets, ½ ounce. Add continuously, as needed, depending on the number of swimmers	Place sticks in skimmer basket; place tablets in floating dispenser or skimmer basket
Calcium hypochlorite; tablets	Chlorine for continuous chlorination; contains no stabilizer	⅓ ounce every 2 days	Place tablets in floating dispenser
Calcium hypochlorite; powder	Chlorine for superchlorination	2 ounces every 2 weeks	Scatter into pool water; allow chlorine reading to drop back to 3 ppm before using pool
Sodium hypochlorite; liquid	Chlorine for superchlorination	1 cup every 2 weeks	Pour into pool water at several points; allow chlorine reading to drop back to 3 ppm before using pool
Sodium bisulphate; powder	Acid for reducing pH level	As indicated by test kit, but no more than 4 ounces per hour	Dilute in water, pour into pool at various places
Muriatic acid (dilute hydrochloric acid); liquid	Acid for reducing pH level; cheaper than sodium bisulphate	As indicated by test kit, but no more than 3¼ fluid ounces per hour	Apply directly, without diluting; use great caution when handling to avoid burns
Muriatic acid; liquid	Acid for reducing total alkalinity	1 ounce to lower alkalinity by 4 ppm; no more than 3¼ fluid ounces per hour	Apply directly without diluting; use caution; if application lowers pH reading below optimum level, compensate with pH increaser
Sodium carbonate, also called soda ash; powder	Alkaline salt for raising pH level	As indicated by test kit, but no more than 2½ ounces per hour	Scatter into pool water
Sodium bicarbonate, also called baking soda; powder	Alkaline salt for raising total alkalinity	As indicated by test kit	Scatter into pool; if application raises pH reading above optimum level, compensate with pH reducer
Trihydroxytriazene; powder	Stabilizer for chlorine	As indicated by professional analysis	Scatter into pool water
Quaternary ammonium compounds; liquid	Wetting agent for preventing algae	Initial dose 2½ fluid ounces; continuing dose ⅖ fluid ounce	Pour into water along sides of pool
Sodium dichloro-s-triazenetrione, also called sodium dichloroisocyanurate; powder	Chlorine for normal chlorination of hot tubs	As indicated by test kit; use 1/10 ounce to raise chlorine reading by .5 ppm	Sprinkle into water

Choosing the right chemical. Use the table above to select the kind and amount of chemical needed for routine maintenance and to correct imbalances in the water chemistry. Read down to find chemicals indicated by their generic names and by form—liquid, powder or solid. Read across to find their purpose, proper dosage and method of application. Where several chemicals are listed for the same job, choose the one that you find most convenient. Where dosages are recommended, amounts are for 1,000 U.S. gallons of water; make adjustments for the size of your pool or hot tub. For example, use 20 times the amount shown here if you have a 20,000-gallon pool, half the amount for a 500-gallon hot tub or spa.

To determine the water volume of your pool, consult the builder who installed it or the instruction manual. You can also calculate the volume yourself. For a rectangular pool, multiply the length by the width by the average depth (all measurements in feet); then multiply the result by 7.5 to get the number of U.S. gallons. For an oval pool multiply the length by the width by the average depth, then multiply the result by 5.9. For a round pool, multiply the diameter by itself, then by the average depth, then by 5.9. If you have a free-form pool, multiply the square footage of the surface by the average depth times 7.5. Raise your estimate if the recommended chemical dosages consistently have too little effect; lower it if they have too much.

Machines that Clean Pool Water

Although chemicals keep pool water germ-free and noncorrosive, a mechanical filtration system is needed to remove dirt and dust, thus keeping the water clear. Crystalline water, besides being attractive, is a safety feature: A swimmer in trouble must be seen clearly to be rescued quickly.

Most of the work of scouring the water clean is done by a filter, generally one of three common types. The simplest is the sand filter, which consists of a large container filled two-thirds full of sand. Pipes and a pump deliver water under pressure to the top of the container. As the water makes its way between grains of sand, the dirt is trapped.

A second filtration method uses a lightweight sandlike material called diatomaceous earth or diatomite. This material is mixed with water to form a slurry that is fed through the pool pump into a filtration vessel containing fine-mesh screens. The diatomite catches in the screens, coating them. In operation, the pool water is pumped through the diatomite, which traps dirt particles.

A relatively new method of filtration uses cylindrical cartridges holding pleated filter membranes. The cartridges, similar in construction to those in automobile air cleaners, are arranged in a tank. Water pumped into the tank passes through the cartridges and emerges clean.

Although any one of these filter systems can be run continuously without harm, operating the pump only part time saves electricity and still does an adequate cleaning job. Thus, many pools have timer switches connected to the pump motor. To set a timer, start by running the filter 10 hours a day. Observe how well the clarity of the water is maintained—you should always be able to see clearly the main drain on the pool bottom. Then adjust the running time until you find an acceptable minimum.

Eventually, the filter becomes clogged and must be cleaned—a condition disclosed by high readings on a pressure gauge. Clean a sand or diatomite filter by reversing the flow of water and draining it away or straining it for return to the pool. Clean a system with cartridge-type filters by opening the filter tank and hosing off its elements.

In many pools the filter system is connected to a heater that warms the pool water. When the filter is being cleaned, this boiler should be turned off, since water will no longer be flowing through it and the unit could burn out.

Caution should also be observed in bringing the water up to the correct level for the filter system to operate properly. This level—usually halfway up the skimmer opening—is constantly being reduced through evaporation, splashing or backwashing. Some pools have fill spouts, but if you must use a garden hose, be sure to keep its end out of the water. Otherwise, a drop in water pressure could cause pool water to be siphoned into the pipes of your house. While pool water is theoretically drinkable, in many localities it is illegal to fill a pool by dangling a garden hose into it.

Anatomy of a filter assembly. In the normal operating cycle of this diatomite filter (*orange arrows*), water is drawn from the pool by the pump and then passes through the center portion of a cylindrical valve and into the filter. Filtered water passes back through the upper portion of the valve and returns to the pool. At the top of the filter, a pressure gauge indicates when the filter is congested and needs backwashing, and an air-relief valve allows excess air to be drawn from the filter manually. In the backwashing cycle (*green arrows*), which you start by lifting the handle atop the cylindrical valve, water flow is reversed, entering the filter through the upper portion of the cylindrical valve and then traveling through the lower portion of the valve to the separation tank, where the dirt and used diatomite are strained out. The cleansed water then passes through the tank and back to the pool.

In the system shown here, a pool-cleaning pump draws water from the return pipe to operate an automatic pool-cleaning device that floats on the water. A small circuit-breaker panel nearby has breakers for the pool pump, the pool-cleaner pump and the pool lights. Two timers control the pool-pump and pool-cleaner motors.

PRESSURE GAUGE
AIR-RELIEF VALVE
FILTER
CYLINDRICAL VALVE
TIMER
CIRCUIT-BREAKER PANEL
SEPARATION TANK
SIGHT GLASS
PUMP
POOL-CLEANER PUMP
TO POOL
FROM POOL
TO POOL CLEANER

Operating a timer. Set the timer to run the filter pump for a specific number of hours at the time of day you prefer. First, loosen the setscrew on the ON tripper at the edge of the dial and slide the tripper until it aligns with the time of day you want the pump to start; tighten the setscrew. Next, align the OFF tripper with the desired hour for the pump to turn off, and tighten the tripper setscrew. Finally, set the timer to the exact time of day by rotating the dial underneath the fixed pointer until the correct time lies directly beneath the pointer.

Additional pairs of trippers stored at the base of the timer can be attached to the dial to break the total running time into segments. A manual switch lets you turn the pump on and off.

Cleaning the pump strainer. Once a week shut down the filter system by turning off the timer at its manual switch and flipping off the pump's circuit breaker. Remove the strainer lid on top of the pump, lift out the strainer basket and empty it. Replace the basket, fill the basket receptacle with water and fasten down the lid. Switch the pump on and open the air-relief valve on the top of the filter tank, to release any air that entered the tank during this operation. When water squirts from the valve, close it.

In some filtration systems, the pipes leading to and from the pool have gate valves. Shut these off before removing the strainer lid and open them before restarting the pump.

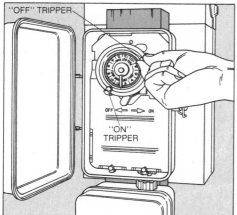

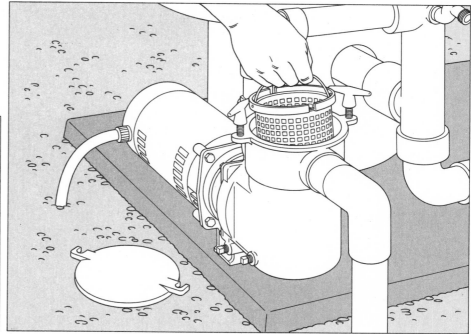

Cleaning a Diatomite Filter

1 **Reversing the filter valve.** If the filtration system has a separation tank, open the gate valve of the tank. Otherwise, connect a hose to the system's backwash outlet. Clean and restart the pump, then begin backwashing by lifting a plunger handle on top of the cylinder valve or by setting a rotary valve to BACKWASH. Watch the sight glass until the water runs clear—usually in about 3 minutes. Stop and start the pump several times to flush out any remaining dirt. Add water to diatomite in a bucket and pour the mixture into the skimmer. Use one 2-pound coffee can full of diatomite to every 5 square feet of filter area, as listed on the filter specification plate. Return the cylindrical filter valve to its normal operating position and close the gate valve of the separation tank. Note the reading on the pressure gauge atop the filter tank; the system will need backwashing again when the reading is 10 pounds higher, usually after several weeks.

Some diatomite filters have a lever on the top of the filter tank that lets you shake the filter screens inside without opening the cover. To use this device, follow the maker's directions.

2 **Cleaning out the separation tank.** Turn off the pump, open the air-relief valve on the top of the separation tank, then loosen the metal band that holds together the top and bottom sections of the tank. Pull off the top section. Remove the strainer bag from inside the tank, turn it inside out into a trash can and then rinse the bag with a garden hose. Drain the tank by removing its drain cap. Replace the cap, strainer bag, tank top and metal band, and close the air-relief valve. Caution: Be sure the top is securely clamped, or it may blow off when the pump is started. Restart the pump and vent any air from the filter tank by opening its air-relief valve.

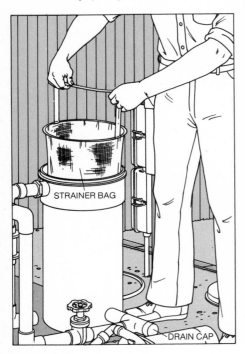
STRAINER BAG
DRAIN CAP

Backwashing a Sand Filter

Setting a rotary valve. Clean the pump's strainer basket as shown on page 119 and, if necessary, attach a hose to the filter drain. With the pump on, set a rotary valve to the BACKWASH position. Watch the sight glass on the back of the valve until the water runs clear—this will take about 3 minutes. Rotate the valve to the RINSE position, if one is provided, and again watch the sight glass until the water runs clear. Return the valve to the FILTER position. If the filter is equipped with a cylindrical rather than a rotary valve, lift the valve handle until the water runs clear in the sight glass, then lower it. Finally, note the reading on the pressure gauge; after several weeks, when the reading is about 8 pounds higher, backwash the system again.

ROTARY VALVE

Cleaning a Cartridge Filter

Rinsing the filter elements. With the pump off, the filter-tank air-relief valve open and any gate valves closed on the supply and return pipes, clean the strainer basket as shown on page 119. Unfasten and remove the top of the filter tank, open the drain valve, and hose down the filter elements to remove dirt. If the filter tank has no drain valve, remove the filter-element assembly for rinsing. Close the drain valve or replace the filter elements in the tank; replace and fasten the top. Caution: Be sure the top is securely clamped, or it may blow off when the pump is started. Turn on the pump and open any gate valves; when water squirts out the air-relief valve, close it. Rinse the elements again after a week, or when the reading is about 6 pounds higher; check the owner's manual.

Preparing a Pool for Winter Cold

If you live in an area where winter temperatures drop below freezing, your pool and its plumbing must be given special protection from cold. While the pool itself—whether above- or below-ground—is left filled at a slightly lower level, all water must be removed from the filtration system, pool cleaner, heater and their pipes. Then the pool must be protected with a cover held down against the apron with water-filled bags. Both cover and bags can be purchased from a pool-supply store.

The job of winterizing a pool begins with a late-fall vacuuming and brushing of the pool interior. If you have a separate pool cleaner, remove the floating element but leave its hoses, if any, stretched out full length along the pool bottom. Detach ladders by loosening the bolts that hold them in place, and store them out of the weather. Prepare each pool light for winter according to the manufacturer's instructions, which vary with the design of the light.

Partially drain the pool through its filter system to a level 4 inches below the skimmer opening. If you have a sand or diatomite filter system, drain the pool by setting the skimmer's flow control to the main drain, setting and running the filter in its backwashing mode only until the water drops to the desired level. If you have a diatomite filter with a separation tank—an accessory that normally returns the filtered water to the pool—reverse the action of the tank by attaching a hose to the separation-tank drain and closing the gate valve on the tank's return pipe. If your pool has a cartridge-filter system, drain the pool by closing the gate valve on the filter's return pipe and attaching a garden hose to the drain faucet on the pipe. The faucet is then opened, the pump turned on and the water lifted from the pool.

After the pool has been drained to its winter level, the water should be given one final superchlorination treatment and one final application of wetting agent to carry it through to spring, when the winterizing procedure is reversed.

1 Emptying the filter system. With the pump off and the gate valves closed on the pipes leading to and from the pool, open all the plugs, caps and valves that drain the filtration system. Usually there are two for the filter pump, one or two for the pool heater, and one each for the filter tank, the separation tank and the pool-cleaner attachment. Each will be on the unit itself or on a pipe close by. Open and hose out the interiors of the filter tank and the separation tank on diatomite or cartridge filter systems; rinse the filter parts and empty the strainer bag of the separation tank. Use a sponge to remove the last of the water from the tanks.

When the system has emptied, coat the threading of drain plugs and caps with pipe compound or tape. Then cap or plug all the drain openings in the filter system except one—leave one drain open on the pump.

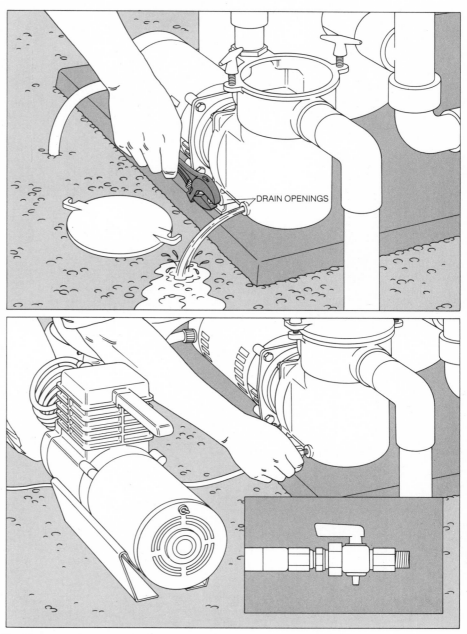

DRAIN OPENINGS

2 Hooking up an air compressor. In preparation for blowing out the pipes leading to the pool, attach a rented air compressor to the filter pump. To adapt the end of the compressor hose to the pump, use a swivel fitting, valve and ¼-inch pipe-thread fitting (inset).

3 **Installing the freeze plugs.** Insert a rubber freeze plug (inset), available at pool-supply stores, into the end of each return pipe along the sides of the pool. Turn the wing nut on each plug to expand the rubber portion until it fits tight against the inside of the pipe.

4 **Sealing the skimmer.** Slide a properly sized freeze plug down through the neck of the skimmer into the pipe coming from the main drain. Tighten the wing nut on the plug, using a homemade wrench—a length of ¾-inch plastic pipe with a T-connector handle at one end and a notch to fit the wing nut at the other. Seal off the neck of the skimmer with a slightly larger freeze plug, then empty the skimmer.

In some skimmers the openings to pipes from the main drain and to the filter pump are side by side in the bottom of the skimmer rather than offset as shown here. Both should be closed with freeze plugs of the appropriate size.

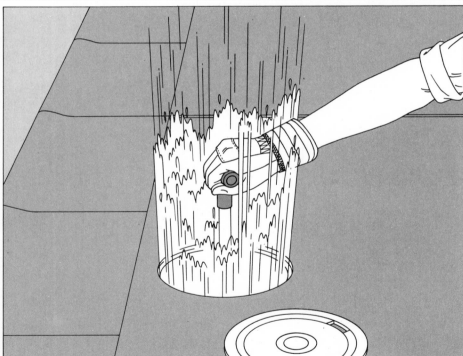

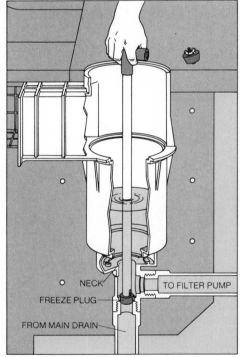

FREEZE PLUG

NECK

FREEZE PLUG

FROM MAIN DRAIN

TO FILTER PUMP

5 **Blowing out the lines.** Run the compressor until the filter-tank pressure gauge reads 20 pounds. Remove the freeze plug in the neck of the skimmer, using the homemade T wrench. (On a dual-opening skimmer, remove the plug on the pipe leading to the filter pump.) Caution: When this plug comes off, it will release a geyser of water and pressurized air; keep your face away from the top of the skimmer and protect your wrench hand with a glove. When the geyser stops, reinsert the plug and allow the pressure to build up again. Continue reinserting and releasing the plug until no more water emerges with the air. Then tighten the plug for the last time and remove any water in the skimmer.

Repeat the procedure for each of the return-pipe openings around the top of the pool and for the pool-cleaner pipe. Although some of these pipes may be below water level, the continuously running compressor will keep the pipes clear after the water in them has been blown out. When all the pipes are clear, disconnect the compressor and plug the one drain in the filter pump that remained open. If the filter system has no housing, cover it loosely with a tarpaulin.

Fending Off Frost Damage with a Cover and Pump

1 **Putting the pool under cover.** Line the perimeter of the pool with the empty water bags to be used for weighting down the cover and fill them with water, leaving some space for the water to expand as it freezes. Place the cover, folded accordion-fashion, at one end of the pool and anchor it with water bags. With a helper, gradually unfold the cover, drawing it down the sides of the pool. Fold any excess under; roll water bags onto all edges of the cover.

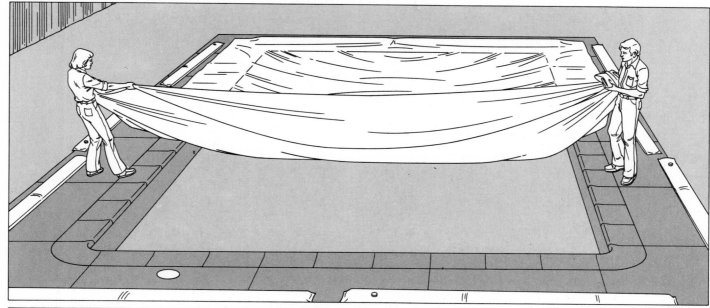

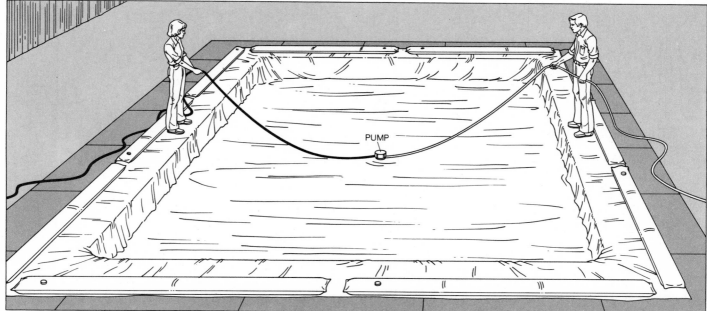

PUMP

2 **Freeing the cover of standing water.** Periodically during the winter, siphon the accumulated water and melted snow from the top of the pool cover with a small submersible pump. Position the pump at the center of the cover and use the pump hose to whip the unit upright while a helper holds the electric cord, as yet unplugged. Turn the pump on as needed, taking care not to operate it when the pool cover is dry.

In spring remove the pump and the pool cover, sweep the pool cover free of debris, let it dry and fold it up accordion-fashion for storage. Wash and empty the water bags.

Tapping Nature for a Fishing Pond All Your Own

Today no one needs to wait for a melting glacier to form a natural pond. If you own enough land and have access to a reliable source of water, you can build your own pond and stock it with fish or outfit it with docks for swimming and boating. Fortunately, you can turn over much of the work, inexpensively and confidently, to experts. The local agent of the Soil Conservation Service will probably, at no charge, survey your land and help you design a pond that fits both your needs and the site conditions. Often this agent will also recommend a reputable bulldozer operator or dragline excavator for the construction.

But even though you can entrust many of the engineering and construction details to experts, it is important that you too understand the basic requirements and options of pond construction—so that you can anticipate the design problems and oversee the work.

The most obvious requirement for any pond is a source of water. Streams, springs, ground water within the earth, and surface runoff from rain and snow—either alone or in combination—are typically used to fill ponds. As essential as any of these, however, is a basin that will retain the water. Clay and silty clay, for instance, are ideal soil types for pond bottoms. But never put a pond over limestone bedrock, because crevices in the rock will quickly drain out the water.

Any pond design should provide for a fairly constant water level, even through drought and flood. The soil conservationist will probably be able to suggest specific tactics for this, taking into account both the sources of water and the topography of the land.

In any pond that depends largely on surface runoff for its fill, the land area that delivers the runoff must be adequate to do the job but not so large that water from storms and spring thaws will undermine and wash out the banks of the pond. And for any pond that relies on water from a stream—through either damming or diversion—you should consider leveling rises and depressions in the surrounding land to protect the pond during floods, and digging outlets called spillways to carry off overflow.

In addition to these on-site factors, lo-cal water laws may influence the design of your pond. These vary from state to state, some states requiring only a building permit, others protecting downstream water rights by prohibiting the damming of a stream or creek. Again, your Soil Conservation Service agent can tell you where to get information on water-use laws as well as any laws governing your liability if someone is injured in your pond.

Once the pond has been designed and its specifications mapped on paper, you can hire a contractor with heavy earthmoving equipment to do the actual excavating and building—preferably someone with pond-building experience. If your pond lies along a stream whose waters are to be diverted by a system of pipes, try to find a plumbing supplier knowledgeable on the subject of pond drainage. If you arrange to have the pipes delivered before excavation begins, the excavator will probably lay them.

Plan to be on the site when the pond is constructed—the engineering design is worthless if the construction is not done properly. Make sure that valuable topsoil is stripped from the pond basin—and from any dam site—and piled to one side. If a dam is constructed, see that it is compacted in layers, without trees, brush or sod clumps, any of which would decay and leave holes for water to pass through. As pipes are connected, watch that they are sealed properly, with either welded joints or watertight metal bands.

As soon as the pond is built, seed the surrounding area with grass to control erosion and silting. Take special care to maintain the grass on any spillways and dams in good condition, since it helps keep fissures and cracks from developing. After heavy rains, fill any holes in spillways and dams with compacted soil and reseed it immediately, if possible. If the soil is frozen, top it with straw to check erosion until you can reseed.

As with any body of water, ponds should be outfitted with lifesaving equipment—buoys, ropes, planks and long poles—and all persons who will use the pond should be familiar with safety rules to govern their use.

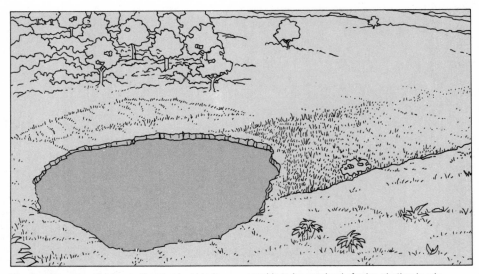

Digging for water. To create the simplest kind of pond, excavate a pit to a level below the water table and allow ground water to fill it. Ideally you should locate this type of pond at the base of a hill, where surface runoff from rain and snow can also contribute to it. If you plan to use the pond for fishing and your area has freezing temperatures, dig the pond deep enough for fish to survive under the ice—usually about 6 feet, but deeper in climates with severe winters. If the pond is to be used only for ice skating in winter and as a wildlife refuge in summer, a depth of 3 to 4 feet is adequate.

In this example, the excavated soil is piled on one side—at least 12 feet away from the bank of the pond and no more than 3 feet high—where it serves as a windbreak. You could also distribute the soil into a gradual slope, as a landscaping element, or pay to have it hauled away.

Damming water for a pond. The commonest way to make a pond is to impound water behind an earth dam built across a stream or creek. The dam itself is made in most cases from layers of earth that have been removed from the pond site and then compacted. Since the compacting is done by a bulldozer, the dam should be designed to be wide enough across the top to support the bulldozer tracks. The back of the dam should slope gently enough to permit the use of a power mower. Beneath the dam, a trench filled with clay soil prevents water from seeping under the dam.

A dammed pond needs one or more outlets, or spillways, to carry off excess water during heavy rains without damage to the dam. In this example, the spillway is a grass-seeded swale that exits from the pond near the dam and 2 feet below its top, and re-enters the stream below the pond. The spillway should be wide enough so that even heavy flooding does not raise the water level enough to erode its sides or to allow large fish to pass through it.

A system of pipes and valves controls the water level in the pond and can be used to drain the pond for cleaning. On the pond side of the dam a vertical pipe, called a riser, is set in a concrete footing and topped by a special metal trap that keeps debris from clogging it. When the water gets too high, it spills over the top of the riser into a horizontal pipe that runs through the dam into the stream on the other side. Inside the dam, one or more rectangular pieces of metal, known as antiseep collars, fit around the horizontal pipe to help prevent leakage around the pipe. Finally, a drainage valve at the base of the riser—here, a gate valve operated by a wheel above water—lets you drain the pond completely.

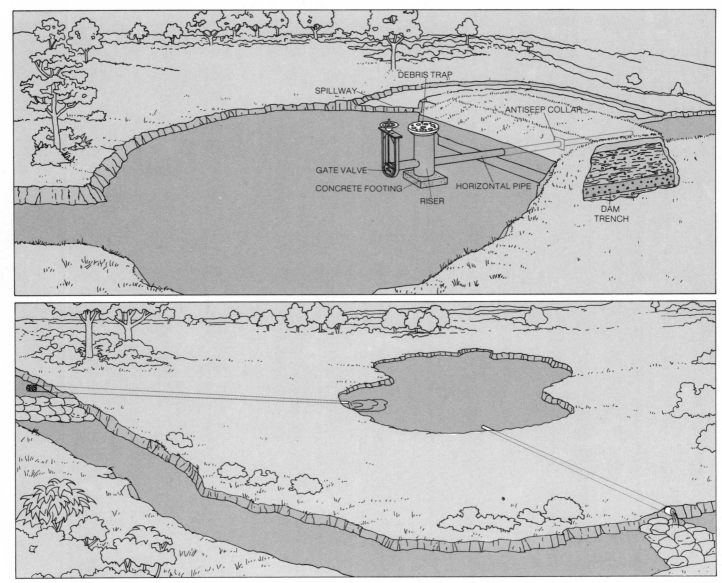

Diverting water for a pond. If water-rights laws in your locality prohibit the damming of a stream, you can still divert water from the stream into a pit. This kind of pond requires enough fall from stream to pond and back to stream to feed and empty the pond by gravity flow.

In this example a shallow rock dam upstream pools enough water for the pipe that feeds into the pond, but does not interfere with the stream's flow. This pipe, set in a trench and at a slight slope, extends several inches into the pond and is capped at its stream end with a re-

movable screen to block debris. A second pipe, running from the downstream end of the pond to the stream, carries overflow back to the stream. Rocks piled beneath the stream end of the second pipe deflect the returning water to keep it from eroding the stream bed.

Building Lake Floats for Docking or Diving

If you live near a pond, a quiet lake or a sheltered cove, you can have a shoreside pier without the trouble or expense of underwater pilings by building a pier that floats. A floating pier rises and falls with the water level but is always linked to a permanent platform on land. The floating part can be removed for winter storage. With modifications, its design is equally applicable to an offshore swimming raft.

The land structure to which the floating pier is attached is a platform consisting mainly of heavy, pressure-treated timbers that are cut, drilled and handled in much the same way as those for a retaining wall (page 19). Here, however, the timbers are butted horizontally into the graded slope of the shoreline, with only a single timber at the water's edge to hold the others level. For ponds that are shallow near the shore, this land-based platform can be cantilevered so it projects over deeper water. Capped 1¼-inch galvanized-steel pipes anchor the platform to the earth; the pipes can be driven down with a sledge until only their caps protrude, or can be left waist-high to provide posts for a rope railing.

For a pond or lake, the floating pier is made of pressure-treated 2-by-4s and exterior-grade plywood, preferably with a nonskid surface, mounted on rigid plastic foam. It is secured to the platform with chains that ride up and down on traveler bars descending from the platform's front edge. For stability the pier should be at least 4 feet wide (for a swimming raft, page 129, the minimum size is 8 by 8 feet) and the supporting floats should be set as far apart as possible. The pier shown here extends 8 feet out into the water; in large bodies of water, two or more floating units can be linked together, railroad-car style: Threaded rods capped with self-locking nuts connect pairs of eyebolts screwed into the ends of each unit.

The most economical and readily available flotation material is polystyrene rigid foam, often called by its trade name, Styrofoam. In nonpolluted waters, polystyrene foam lasts about five years, and then it is easily replaced. Where oil or chemicals are present in the water, or turbulence is likely, it is better to use hollow floats of rigid polyurethane; these come shaped especially for floating piers.

The two floats for this 4-by-8 pier are made from 10-by-20-inch slabs of polystyrene foam, 7½ feet long, together sufficient to support about 1,000 pounds. To calculate the amount of polystyrene foam needed for piers of other sizes, add the estimated weight of the pier to the estimated weight of the total load—the people and equipment likely to be on it at any one time. For safety, add an additional 50 per cent; then divide by 60 to get the final figure in cubic feet. A pier should ride about 12 inches above the water surface and sink about 1 inch under the weight of each person.

In calm water the floating pier needs no other anchoring than the chains that slide along the traveler bars. To counter wave action or storm turbulence, however, extra anchors may be needed. These anchors are 5-gallon cans, full of concrete and with an eyebolt protruding from each top. Each weighs about 100 pounds on land, 55 pounds underwater. Normally they are set beneath the pier corners to be out of the way of swimmers, but for increased stability they can be set away from the pier and farther out from shore. A permanent sign on the pier should warn swimmers of their presence.

The edges of a floating pier or raft are easier on swimmers and boats if ringed with fenders of old fire hose or commercially available marine bumpers, tacked to the frame. Three coats of deck enamel covering all exposed wood parts of the pier help to prevent splinters.

Constructing a Floating Pier

1 **Building the land structure.** Construct a 4-by-8 shoreline platform from eight 6-by-6 timbers, 8 feet long, joining them by bolting two 2-by-6s across the timber ends, front and back; center one bolt in each timber, for a total of eight bolts across each end of the platform. Rest the platform on a shoreline timber to bring it level with the graded land behind, and secure it to the ground by driving four 1¼-inch capped pipes through holes drilled with a brace and auger bit through the timbers. Make sure the holes at the rear of the platform clear the joining bolts, and position the holes at the front of the platform to match holes drilled through the shoreline timber. Drive the pipes at least 2 feet into the ground.

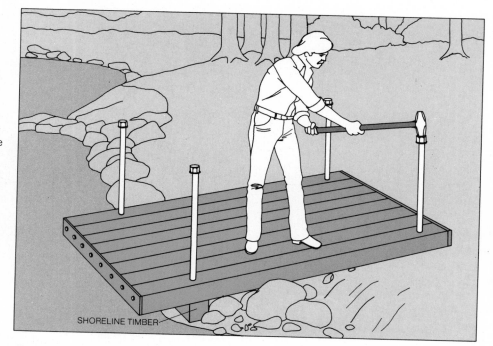

SHORELINE TIMBER

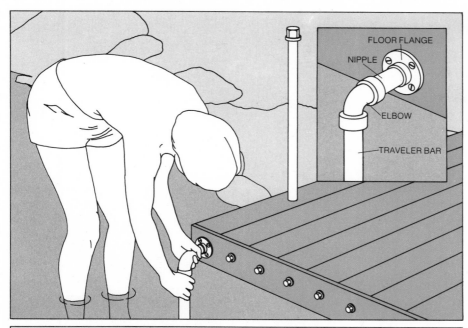

2 **Assembling traveler bars.** Attach two 1¼-inch floor flanges to the front edge of the platform, directly over the end bolts. Screw nipples into them, then 90° elbows (*inset*), and finally, two straight lengths of pipe that reach deep enough into the water so the connecting chains cannot slide off the bottoms. The length of the nipples depends on how far apart you want the pier and platform to be; for a 6-inch gap, use nipples about 2½ inches long.

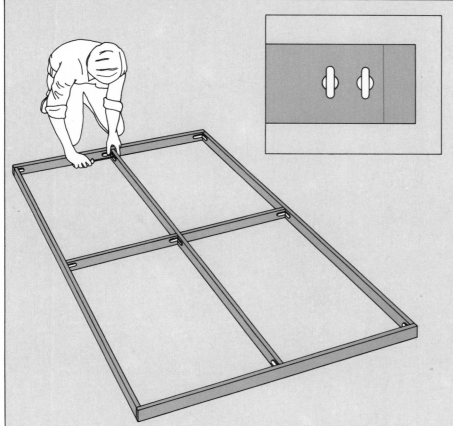

3 **Making the pier frame.** Build a 4-by-8-foot frame of 2-by-4s, using galvanized nails; at all joints, add galvanized angle irons.

Nail a 4-by-8 sheet of plywood to the frame. At each end of the outside face of one 4-foot side of the frame (*inset*), screw in two eyebolts 1½ inches apart; the midpoint of each pair of eyebolts should be 3 inches in from the corner of the frame. On the inside face of the other 4-foot side of the frame, screw in a single eyebolt 12 inches in from each corner of the frame.

4 **Attaching supports for rigid foam.** Nail two pairs of 1-by-6s, 8 feet long, to the underside of the frame, positioning the first board of each pair 5 inches in from a long edge of the frame. Nail the second board of each pair in place 3 inches away from the first.

127

5 **Securing the rigid foam.** Center a 10-by-20-inch slab of rigid foam, 7½ feet long, on each pair of 1-by-6s, positioning the slab so it is flush with the end of the frame containing the two pairs of eyebolts, and is 6 inches short of the end containing the inward-facing eyebolts. Push three pairs of 14-inch threaded rods through each foam slab—a pair at the center and a pair 1 foot in from each end. Mark their positions and drill holes for them in the 1-by-6s. Drill similar holes through 1-by-4 blocks, one block for each of the 12 rods, then secure the foam slabs to the pier with the threaded rods, blocks, washers and nuts.

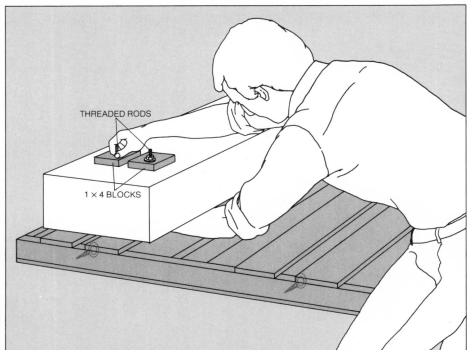

THREADED RODS

1 × 4 BLOCKS

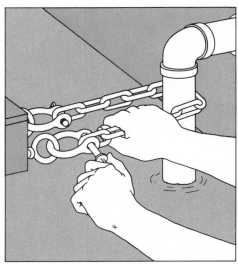

6 **Linking the pier and platform.** Place the floating pier in the water, so the end with the two pairs of eyebolts faces the shore. Shackle one end of a chain to one eyebolt of a pair, loop the chain around the traveler bar and shackle the chain's other end to the second eyebolt. Repeat this procedure for the other traveler bar and pair of eyebolts. Attach a fender to each of the three open sides of the floating pier.

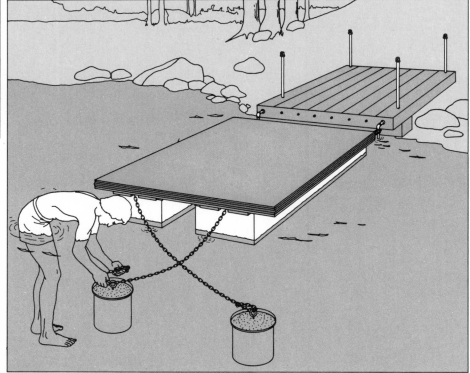

7 **Anchoring the outer end.** Attach chains to the two inward-facing eyebolts, cross the chains underwater and shackle each to an eyebolt protruding from a concrete-filled 5-gallon can. In relatively calm water, set the cans beneath the pier corners; for greater resistance to storms, set them farther apart and farther from shore.

Making a Swimming Raft

1 **Making the frame.** Construct an 8-by-8-foot frame, using 2-by-6s for the sides and crossribs and either 4-by-6s or nailed-together pairs of 2-by-6s for the central spine. Reinforce all joints with angle irons. Nail on two sheets of 4-by-8 plywood, placed so that the seam between them falls over the frame's central spine.

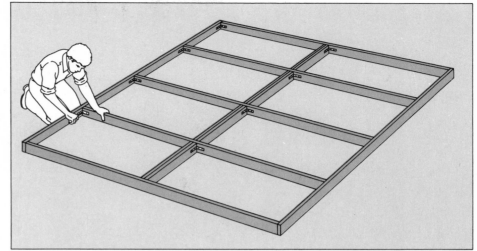

2 **Adding foam floats.** With a helper, turn the structure over, and attach four pairs of 1-by-6s to support the rigid foam, two pairs along the sides and two at evenly spaced intervals in the center. Position these supports parallel with the central spine. Then attach four 8-foot-long slabs of rigid foam. Screw a single eyebolt to the inside face of the 2-by-6 frame.

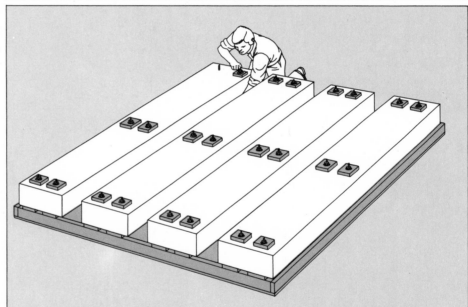

3 **Anchoring the float.** Run a chain through the eyebolts in two concrete-filled 5-gallon cans and shackle them together, then run one end of the chain to the float and shackle it to the float's eyebolt. Attach a fender all around the float.

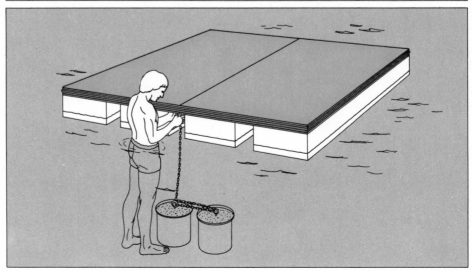

Laying Out Courts and Fields

Layouts for the most popular lawn, pavement and field games are detailed below, based on rules adopted by the organizations identified with each sport. If you consider it essential that you have a regulation court that is absolutely up-to-date, check these dimensions with the organization listed—changes in the playing rules sometimes affect layouts.

Wherever appropriate, the layout includes a recommendation for the amount of free space—called back space—that should surround a playing area. But often you will need to adapt the regulation design to the available space. Where possible, guidelines for such changes—usually reduced areas—are given.

You should orient most game areas on a north-south axis to minimize sun glare. There are two general exceptions: Croquet can be set up in any direction; and areas for games that are played primarily during the fall, such as soccer, should run northwest-southeast.

Shuffleboard (National Shuffleboard Association). On a regulation concrete shuffleboard court, the boundary lines, dead lines, triangles and figures are marked with black shoe dye or acrylic paint. Lines can be between ¾ and 1½ inches wide, except those of the separation triangles, which should be ¼ inch wide. Marked dimensions extend to the center of the lines except at the edges of the court, where they extend to the outside edges of the lines. If your space is limited, you can shorten the court somewhat, but the width should remain the same.

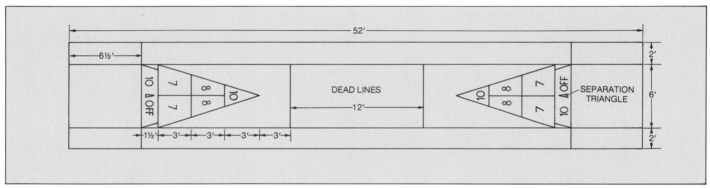

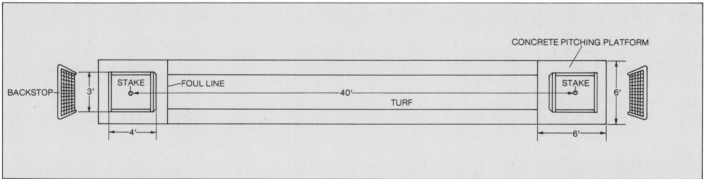

Horseshoes (National Horseshoe Pitchers' Association of America). On a regulation horseshoe court, a 34-foot-long turf field stretches between 6-foot-square concrete pitching platforms. In the center of each platform a 3-by-4-foot clay-filled box contains a 1-inch steel stake, 14 inches high and slanted 3 inches toward the center of the field; the distance between the bases of the stakes is 40 feet. In a tournament court, a concrete walkway borders the turf field on each side, a 2-foot-high backstop behind each stake keeps the shoes from bouncing out of play, and the back space extends at least 2 feet on each side of the court.

For a backyard game, you can simply set two stakes on level ground, 40 feet apart or less.

Croquet (National Croquet Association, Inc.). On an American regulation croquet court, 10 wickets, each only slightly larger than the ball, are set up in the configuration shown. In the more common and less demanding backyard court, nine larger wickets are set up in the same basic pattern but distances are scaled to available space. Generally the first wicket is placed a mallet-handle length away from the starting stake and the second wicket a mallet-handle length beyond the first. The stake and wickets at the opposite end of the court are set up in the same way, then the remaining wickets are positioned symmetrically between, with one wicket instead of two in the center of the court.

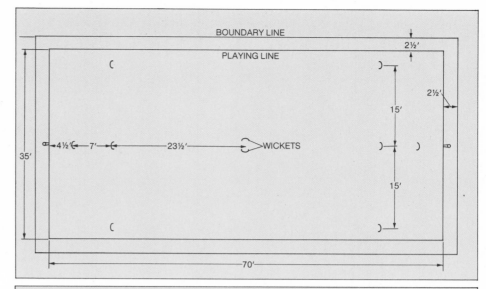

Badminton (American Badminton Association). On a regulation court for competition badminton, 1½-inch-wide lines mark the court area as shown. All measurements extend to the outside edges of the lines, except the ones for the center service line; these measurements end in the middle. Official rules call for a net height of 61 inches at each post and 60 inches in the center. A minimum back space of 6 feet on each side of the court should be provided.

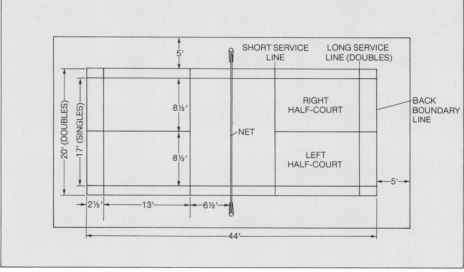

Volleyball (United States Volleyball Association). A regulation volleyball court is marked with 2-inch-wide lines. All measurements extend to the outside of these lines except for those to the center line, which end in the middle. Regulations specify a net height at center court of 95⅝ inches for men and 88⅛ inches for women, with no more than a ¾-inch increase in height at the posts. Rules also require at least 10 feet of back space on each of the four sides of the court. For a backyard court, you can reduce the size to a minimum of 20 feet wide by 40 feet long and lower the net a foot or two.

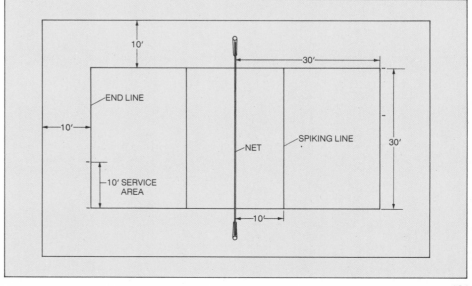

Paddle tennis (United States Paddle Tennis Association). The regulation court for paddle tennis is laid out with 2-inch-wide lines. All measurements extend to the outsides of these lines except those to the center service line, which end in the middle of the line. Regulations specify a net height of 31 inches at each post, with no more than a 1-inch sag in the middle. They also call for a minimum back space of 15 feet at the ends and 10 feet at the sides of the court.

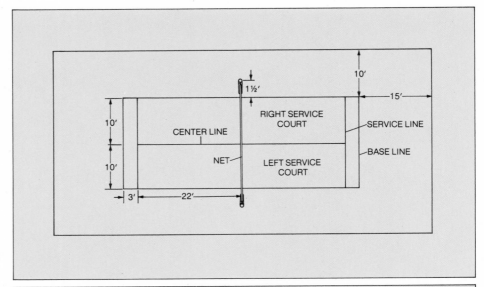

Tennis (United States Tennis Association). The regulation tennis court is marked off by lines 2 inches wide. All measurements extend to the outside edges of the lines except for those to the center service line, which end in the middle of the line. Regulation net height is 42 inches at each post and 36 inches in the center. Although the regulations call for 21 feet of back space on the ends and 12 feet of back space on the sides, if your space is limited you can shorten these distances by 3 feet.

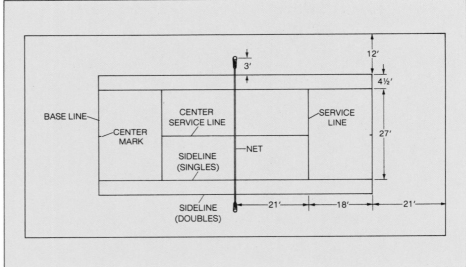

Basketball (National Collegiate Athletic Association). This full-court layout shows measurements for a collegiate-sized basketball court and, in parentheses, gives reduced dimensions for a high-school court. With the exception of the 12-by-8-inch neutral-zone marks, all the lines are 2 inches wide; the lane-space marks are 8 inches long. All measurements extend to the inside edges of the lines. If you install a rectangular backboard, set its lower edge 9 feet above the court surface; if you use a fan-shaped backboard, set its lower edge 9 feet 9 inches above the court surface.

A half-court area is adequate for practice. You may be able to mount a net and backboard on a garage and use the driveway as a playing area.

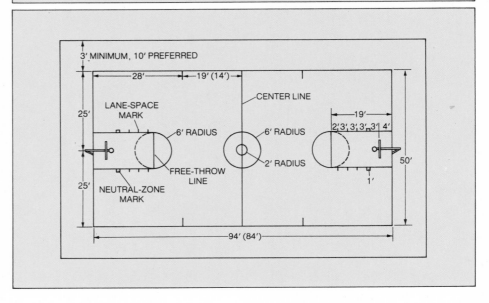

Softball (Amateur Softball Association of America). The softball field designed for play with a 12-inch ball (measured in circumference, not diameter) is marked off with chalk lines that are 2 to 3 inches wide. For fast-pitch softball, the distance from home plate to the fence is 225 feet; for slow-pitch, in which the pitched ball arcs, the distance is 275 feet for men and 250 feet for women.

For softball played with a ball 16 inches in circumference, the distance from the home plate to the pitcher should be 38 feet, the base lines 55 feet long for men and 50 feet long for women, and the distance from home plate to the fence 250 feet for men and 200 feet for women.

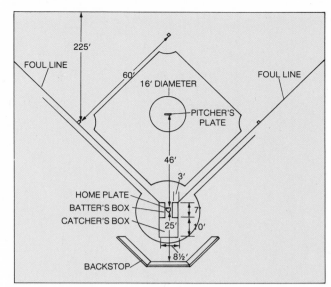

Soccer (National Collegiate Athletic Association). A regulation soccer field is marked off by lines 2 inches wide, with all of the measurements extending to the inside edges of these lines. A goal 8 feet high and 24 feet wide is centered at each end of the playing field.

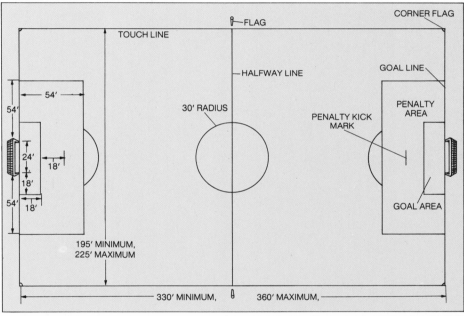

Touch football (The Athletic Institute). The field used for both touch football and a variation, touch-and-flag football, is 100 yards long, with four 20-yard zones and two 10-yard end zones. This field is marked off by lines 4 inches wide, with all measurements extending to the inside edges of these lines. A goal 10 feet high and 23 feet 4 inches wide is centered at each end of the field. A red or orange flexible pylon 18 inches high is placed at each end of each goal line.

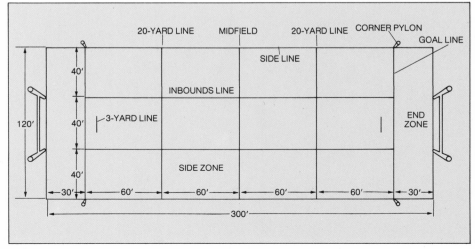

Picture Credits

Credits for pictures from left to right are separated by semicolons, from top to bottom by dashes. The drawings were created by Jack Arthur, Laszlo Bodrogi, Roger C. Essley, Fred Holz, Dick Lee, Joan S. McGurren, W. F. McWilliam and John Martinez.

Cover: Fil Hunter. 6: Fil Hunter. 9-11: Eduino Pereira. 12, 13: Terry Atkinson. 15-23: Ray Skibinski. 24: Fil Hunter. 27-39: Frederic F. Bigio from B-C Graphics. 40-46: John Massey. 47: W. F. McWilliam. 48: Fil Hunter. 50-53: John Massey. 55-67: Walter Hilmers Jr., HJ Commercial Art. 68-71: Terry Atkinson. 73: Richard B. Oliver, architect. 74: Norman McGrath, David Stiles, designer — David Barnes. 75: Jon Naar, Kent Bloomer, architect. 76, 77: Donald Wall, architect. 78: Lee Lockwood from Black Star, V. Michael Weinmayr, architect — John Neubauer, Lloyd Greenberg and Jeffrey Wilkes, designers. 79: Al Freni, M. Paul Friedberg & Partners, architects. 80: Ron Green, M. Paul Friedberg & Partners, architects. 81: John S. McGurren. 83-93: John Massey. 94: Ted Streshinsky. 96-101: Eduino Pereira. 103-106: Frederic F. Bigio from B-C Graphics. 107-111: Snowden Associates Inc. 112-123: Frederic F. Bigio from B-C Graphics. 124, 125: Gerry Gallagher. 126-129: Forte Inc. 130-133: Elsie Hennig.

Acknowledgments

The index/glossary for this book was prepared by Louise Hedberg. The editors also wish to thank the following: William R. Adams, Soil Conservation Service, Culpeper, Va.; Alexandria Lighting and Supply, Inc., Alexandria, Va.; Amateur Softball Association, Oklahoma City, Okla.; American Shuffleboard Co., Inc., Union City, N.J.; American Soccer League, Inc., New York, N.Y.; Jim Arnoux, Evanston Parks Department, Evanston, Ill.; Arrow Tank Company, Buffalo, N.Y.; Linda Ballard, Fairfax, Va.; Barrel Builders, St. Helena, Calif.; Dr. James B. Beard, Professor of Turf Grass Science, Texas A&M University, College Station, Tex.; Armand Benedek, Bedford Village, N.Y.; Charles A. Bjorson, Rockville, Md.; William Blanton, Marine Structural Applications, Inc., Dumfries, Va.; Kent and Nona Bloomer, Guilford, Conn.; Rick Briggs, Landscape Architect, Collinsville, Ill.; Naud Burnett, Edwin Gerlach, Howard Garrett Inc., Dallas, Tex.; California Cooperage, San Luis Obispo, Calif.; California Hot Tubs, New York, N.Y.; James Chasnovitz, Landscape Architect, Manassas, Va.; Manuel M. Colbert, Belle Haven Country Club, Alexandria, Va.; Geoffrey S. Cornish, Fiddlers Green, Amherst, Mass.; Joseph Cushing, Poly Snow Canada, Ltd., Toronto, Ont., Canada; Dr. Albert del Negro, Georgetown University Medical Center, Washington, D.C.; Alain C. de Vergie, Fort Washington, Md.; Diamond Tool and Horseshoe Co., Duluth, Minn.; M. H. Dickinson, Regency Racquet Club, McLean, Va.; Kurt Donat, Newport Beach, Calif.; R. Wayne Evans, Huntingtown, Md.; John J. Ferguson, General Electric Company, Columbia, Md.; John Finnan, Finnan Wood Tank Company, Rushville, N.Y.; Thomas D. Flinn, Binghamton Brick Co., Binghamton, N.Y.; Larry Freedman, Long Fence Co., Merrifield, Va.; M. Paul Friedberg & Partners, New York, N.Y.; Dick Funkhauser, Har-Tru Corporation, Hagerstown, Md.; Robert G. Goeltz, Potomac, Md.; Goldberg and Rodler, Inc., Huntington, N.Y.; Ray Gordon, Portland Cement Association, Arlington, Va.; Lloyd Greenberg, Washington, D.C.; Thomas Hall, Ice Skating Institute of America, Wilmette, Ill.; Douglas N. Hanson, Republic Steel Corporation, Canton, Ohio; Allen Hardee, Outdoor Sports Ski Shop, Virginia Beach, Va.; Vince Harold, Monsey Products Co., East Rutherford, N.J.; Martin E. Harp, Chief Electrical Inspector, Alexandria, Va.; Richard E. Highfill, Soil Conservation Service, Washington, D.C.; Hot Tubs International, Falls Church, Va.; Hot Tub Works, Alexandria, Va.; Puller A. Hughes Jr., Northern Virginia Soil and Water Conservation District, Fairfax, Va.; Arthur T. Hunsberger, P.E., C.L.S., Hunsberger & Monaco, Fairfax, Va.; David Ingemie, Ski Industries America, Washington, D.C.; International Association of Approved Basketball Officials, W. Hartford, Conn.; Rick Johnson, Sylvania Corporation, Springfield, Va.; Lawrence Kennedy, Thomas A. Edison High School, Alexandria, Va.; Robert Lee, Ron Lewis, John Welborn, Robert Lee Co., Charlottesville, Va.; John Linde, Columbia Cascade Timber Co., Portland, Ore.; William Longenecker, U.S. Dept. of Agriculture, Beltsville, Md.; William P. Markert, National Swimming Pool Institute, Washington, D.C.; Tom Maxwell, Playtime Pools, Woodbridge, Va.; Katherine N. Mergen, Soil Conservation Service, U.S. Dept. of Agriculture, Washington, D.C.; Moody and Company, Inc., Sports Division, Milford, Conn.; National Landscape Association, Washington, D.C.; Thomas J. Nisbet, Ellensburg, Wash.; William O'Brien, Long Fence Company, Capitol Heights, Md.; The Olde Towne Tennis Shop, Alexandria, Va.; Richard B. Oliver, New York, N.Y.; Joseph L. Owens, American Plywood Association, Annandale, Va.; Herbert Palmer, Waterfront Equipment and Hardware Store, Annapolis, Md.; Jim Pendleton, The Good Earth Nursery Inc., Burke, Va.; William Peterson, Division of Parks and Recreation, St. Paul, Minn.; Gene Plattner, Skate On, Inc., Bridgeton, Mo.; Port-A-Slope Corp., Anaheim, Calif.; Richard Priebe, Porter Equipment Company, Schiller Park, Ill.; Guy L. Rando, Reston, Va.; Lloyd and Beverly Rivard, Alexandria, Va.; George Rosenbaum, Middleburg, Va.; David Rowan, Editor and Publisher, *Ski Area Management*, N. Salem, N.Y.; B. H. Runyon Co., Inc., Falls Church, Va.; Richard Schadt Associates, Inc., San Francisco, Calif.; Donald Singer, Ft. Lauderdale, Fla.; Harold Skjelbostad, Inter-Design Inc., Minneapolis, Minn.; Eugene R. Smith & Assoc., Tampa, Fla.; Soccer Supplies of Northern Virginia, Falls Church, Va.; Spring Mountain Cooperage, St. Helena, Calif.; Gerald and Linda Stern, Washington, D.C.; David Stiles, New York, N.Y.; Robert Thomas, Tennis Court Construction Company, Washington, D.C.; Clifford A. Thorpe Jr., Thorpe-Smith Inc., Falls Church, Va.; George P. Toma, Kansas City Chiefs and Royals, Kansas City, Mo.; U.S. Badminton Association, Swartz Creek, Mich.; U.S. Paddle Tennis Association, Brooklyn, N.Y.; U.S. Soccer Federation, New York, N.Y.; U.S.

Tennis Association, Education and Research Division, Princeton, N.J.; U.S. Tennis Court and Track Builders Association, Glenview, Ill.; U.S. Volleyball Association, San Francisco, Calif.; Donald Wall, New Jersey Institute of Technology, Newark, N.J.; Anne M. Wardell, Soil Conservation Service, Fairfax, Va.; M. A. Warnes, American Wood Preservers Institute, McLean, Va.; Theodore H. Webersinn, Interprofessional Planning and Design Studio, Ltd., Silver Spring, Md.; V. Michael Weinmayr, Lexington, Mass.; Ernest Wertheim, San Francisco, Calif.; Jeffrey Wilkes, Washington, D.C.; Wilson Sporting Goods Co., River Grove, Ill.; Roy Winder, U.S. Figure Skating Association, Colorado Springs, Colo. The following persons assisted in the writing of this book: Patricia Baker, Victoria W. Monks, Wendy Murphy.

Index/Glossary

Included in this index are definitions of many of the technical terms used in this book. Page references in italics indicate an illustration of the subject mentioned.

Aerating: *punching holes in compacted soil to admit air and water.* Using aerator, 26, 27

Backstop, building, for tennis court, 60, *61-63*
Badminton: court, *131;* lighting, 54, *55;* poles for, 50; subgrading, 14, *15*
Berm: *low bank of earth on downhill side of drainage depression.* Creating, 22
Boundaries: establishing, 26, 29; of pool, 96; regulation court sizes, *130-133;* setting with transit level, *16-17, 33;* staking area for excavation, 14, *18;* of tennis court, *33*
Boundary lines, marking: circular, *29;* with flexible pylon marker, *30;* on grass, 26, 29, *30;* with liner, *24,* 26, *30;* with paint, 26, *30;* with powder, 26, 29, *30;* on tennis court, *41*
Building codes: and deck, 107; easements, 8; and fences, 8, 32, 66; hot tub, 102; playhouse, 68; and retaining wall, 19; wiring, 54

Circuits: computing power load, 54; and quartz lamps, 54; tapping into, 54, *56. See also* Fixtures; Wiring
Clay: soil, 12, 32, *104;* tennis court, 32, 37, 38, *40,* 42
Concrete: footings for poles, 50, *51,* 82, *89, 91*
Crushed stone: base of tennis court, 32, 35, *36-37;* screeding, *36, 37*

Dam, 124, *125*
Deck: attaching to house, *108;* building, *107-111;* of gym, *83;* of playhouse, *71;* scribing curves in, *109;* stairs to, *110-111;* wood for, 107
Drainage: above-ground pool, 96; on grass field, 26; hot tub, *103,104;* of informal play area, 10; layers of crushed stone, 32, 35, *36-37;* planning, *22;* and playhouse, 68; in putting green, *31;* and retaining wall, 19, *21;* and slope, 14; surface system, *22;* and tennis court, 32; underground systems, 22, *23*
Dry well: *rock- or gravel-filled pit into which excess water drains.* Need for, 22

Earth-moving, 8, 14; preparing field for grading, *16-18;* subgrading with garden tools, *15. See also* Grading
Excavator: hiring professional, 14, 124; preparing grading plan for, 14, *18*

Fence: building wood, 60, *66-67;* fencing materials, 60, 66; gates , 63, 67; safety, 60, 96; setting posts, *50-53;* tennis, 32; tennis-court backstop, 60, *61-63*
Filter pump: above-ground pool, 96, *101;* hot tub, 102, *103;* in-ground pool, *112, 118-122*
Filtration systems of in-ground pool, *112, 118;* backwashing, *119-120;* cartridge, 118, *120,* 121; cleaning, 118, *119-120;* diatomite, *118, 119,* 121; sand, 118, *120;* winterizing, *121-122*
Fixtures: incandescent lighting, *55;* installing, *56-57;* mercury-vapor lamps, 54, *55, 59;* mounting lights on posts, *58-59;* quartz lamps, *48,* 54, *55, 59*
Footings: concrete, *50-51,* 82, 89, *91;* for stairs, *110*
Foundation: hot-tub, 102, *103, 104;* playhouse, 68

Gate: wire fence, *63;* wood fence, *67*
Golf: laying out home course, 31; putting green, *31*
Grading: above-ground pool, *96-98;* fine, *47,* 96; with garden tools, 14, *15;* grading plan, 14, *18;* measuring, 10, 11, 14, 15, *18;* with radial level, *97-98;* and retaining wall, 19; tennis court, 32, *34-35, 47;* with transit level, 6, 14, *16-17, 18,* 36, 37
Grass: around pond, 124; artificial, 81; care of lawn, 26, 27; drainage, 26; laying sod, *28;* marking lines, *24,* 26, *29, 30;* playing surface, 25, 26; putting green, *31;* repairing worn spots, 26, 27; and skating rink, 44; slope, 14; varieties of grasses, 26, 31
Greenstone: dressing, *42, 43;* tennis-court surface, *38-39,* 47
Ground fault interrupter: *sensitive circuit breaker designed for use in damp places, especially outdoors.* Use, 54
Gym, climbing: cargo net, *82, 83;* climbing structures, *78-80;* designing, 72, 82, *83;* fireman's pole, *91;* overhead ladder, *85;* platform, 82, *83-84;* sandbox, *92;* seesaw, *92-93;* sliding board, *86-89;* swinging bridge, *84-85;* tire swing, *90*

Hot tub, *94, 95, 102;* assembling, *104-106;* choosing site, 102; cleaning, 102; filling, 102, foundation, 102, *103, 104;* hoops and lugs, 102, *106;* maintenance, 102; milling wooden parts, 102, *103;* plumbing support system, 102, *103;* precautions, *103;* winterizing, 102. *See also* Deck; Water

Land: checking unknown swimming area, *12;* evaluating yard, 7, *9, 10-13;* mapping and measuring, *10-11;* testing soil, 12, 32
Legal considerations: "attractive nuisance" law, 7; drainage system, 22; water laws, 124; zoning laws, 8, 66. *See also* Building codes
Lighting: children's play area, 49, *55;* installing fixtures, *56-57;* outdoor system, 54, *55;* requirements, 54; wiring fixtures to posts, *58-59*
Liner, marking boundary lines with, *24,* 26, *30*

Measuring property: grade, 10, 11, 14, 15, *18;* mapping outdoor space, 8, *10-11;* plot map, 8
Mercury-vapor lamps, 54, *55, 59*

Net: attaching game nets, 60, 64, *65;* for hockey goal, 44, *46;* rebound, 60, *64-65;* tennis, 38, *40, 41*

Pier, floating, building, *126-128*
Planning: deck, *107;* designing play equipment, 49, *72; 73-80,* 82, *83;* drainage system, *22-23;* grading plan, 14, *18;* hot tub, 102; layout of court, *130-133;* lighting, 54, *55;* mapping and measuring, *10-11;* mock-ups, *11;* new areas, 7, 8, *9-13,* 49; playhouse, *68;* tennis court, 32; yard
Playhouse: building, *68-71;* cutting doors and windows, 68, *69;* examples, *73-77;* foundation, *68;* planning, *68,* 72; safety, 68
Playing field: maintaining grass field, 26, *27-28;* marking lines, *24, 26, 29, 30;* soccer, *133;* softball, *133;* and soil, 12; touch football, *133*
Playing surface: fast-drying court-surfacing materials, 32, *38-39, 42-43,* 47; grass, 8, 14, 25, 26, *27-31;* materials, 25; paved, 14, 32, 34, 37, 38, *40,* 41, 42, *43;* porous, 14, *23,* 32, *35,* 37, 38, *40, 42-43,* 47; synthetic, *81. See also* Grass; Tennis court
Plot map, 8
Pond, construction of, *124-125*
Pool liner, installing, *100-101*
Posts: anchoring metal swing legs, *53;* attaching nets, *65;* for backstop, 50, 60, *61;* in cold regions, 38, 50; deck supports, *107, 108;* fence, *66;* footings for gym, 82, *83-84, 89, 91;* mounting lights on, *58-59;* net, 38, *40;* setting in concrete, 50, *51;* temporary settings for wood posts, 50, *52-53*
Putting green: construction and maintenance, *31*

Quartz lamps, *48,* 54, *55, 59*

Raceway: *channel, usually metal, mounted on surface to hold electrical wires.* Using, 54
Raft, floating swimming, 126, *129*
Railing: on deck, *111;* on playhouse, *71*
Rebar: *steel rods used to reinforce concrete.* Connecting timbers with, *19*
Retaining wall: *reinforced wall for holding back a bank of earth.* Building, *19-21;* drainage, 19, *21;* materials, 19; weep holes, 19, *20, 21*

Screeding: *leveling.* Base of crushed stone, *36, 37;* fast-drying surface, 38, *38-39*
Slope: above-ground pool, 14, 96; establishing for small court, *15;* evaluating for drainage, 9, 10, 14, 22; tennis-court, 14, 32, *34*
Soil: clay, 12, 32, *104;* drainage, 22; and pond bottom, 124; testing, *12,* 32. *See also* Drainage
Sun: and hot tub, 102; orienting playing area, 8, 9, 11, 32, 33, 44, 130
Swale: *shallow drainage channel across slope.* Creating, 22
Swimming pool: automatic cleaning device, *112;* chlorine, 115, *chart* 116, *chart* 117; cleaning, 112, *113;* filtration systems, *112, 118-122;* inspecting, 112; maintenance, *112-123;* patching plaster, *114;* pH level, 115, *chart* 116, *chart* 117; safety, 113; testing and treating water, 115, *116,* 117; using chemicals, 115, *116-117;* winterizing, *121-123*
Swimming pool, above-ground: assembling from kit, 96, *98-101;* cove, *99;* drainage, 96; filter pump, 96, 101; grading site, *96-98;* leveling sand, 96, *99;* liner, *100-101;* repairing liner, 112, *114;* safety fence, 60, 96. *See also* Deck; Water

Tennis court: asphalt, 32, 34, 37, 38, *40,* 41, 42, *43;* base of crushed stone, 32, 35, *36-37;* brick curb, *35;* building, 32, *33-41,* 47; building backstop, 50, 60, *61-63;* clay, 32, 37, 38, *40,* 42; dirt, 32, 37, 38, *40,* 42, 47; drainage, 14, 32; fast-drying, 32, *38-39, 42-43,* 47; gate into enclosed court, *63;* grading, 32, *34-35,* 47; history of game, 25; laying out, 32, *33, 132;* lighting, *55;* maintaining, *42-43;* marking lines, *41;* net posts and anchor, 38, *40,* 50, *52;* porous, watering, 32, 42; rebound net, 60, *64-65;* slope, 14, 32, *34;* surfacing materials, 32, *38-39;* windscreen, 60, *63*
Thatch: *accumulation of mowed grass stems in a lawn.* Removing, 26, *27*
Transit level: *surveying tool used to establish boundaries and measure grades on land surfaces.* Measuring grade, 14, *18, 34,* 36, 37; plotting boundaries, *17, 33;* using, *6, 16-17*
Trees: Drip line, 8, *9;* removing, 32; as windbreak, 8, *9*

Water: drainage systems for, *22, 23;* safety, 95; source of, for pond, *124, 125;* testing and treating, 102, 115, *116,* 117
Water-testing kit, 102, *116*
Weep holes: *gaps in retaining wall that permit drainage.* Planning for, 19, *20, 21*
Wind: and hot tub, 102; patterns, 9, 11; screen, 60, *63;* windbreak, 8, *9*
Wiring: attaching fixtures to posts, *58-59;* computing power load, 54; connecting outdoor box, *57;* installing indoor wall switch, *56;* running UF cable from junction box to outdoors, *58*
Wood: care of, *51;* in deck, *107;* in gym, 82; milling parts for hot tub, 102; preservatives, 19, 51, 107; pressure-treated, 51, 66, 68, 107; sleeves for wooden posts, *52*